TOUGH CHOICES

Bringing Moral Issues Home

Sean Lynch and Brian O'Brien

ave maria press   Notre Dame, IN

Nihil Obstat: The Reverend Theodore Tack, OSA

Imprimatur: The Most Reverend Edward J. Slattery
                       Bishop of Tulsa
                       Given at Tulsa, OK on 2 June 2003

The *Nihil Obstat* and *Imprimatur* are official declarations that a book or pamphlet is free of doctrinal or moral error. No implication is contained therein that those who have granted the Nihil Obstat or Imprimatur agree with its contents, opinions, or statements expressed.

Scripture texts in this work are taken from the *New American Bible with Revised New Testament and Revised Psalms* © 1991, 1986, 1970 Confraternity of Christian Doctrine, Washington, D.C. and are used by permission of the copyright owner. All Rights Reserved. No part of the *New American Bible* may be reproduced without permission in writing from the copyright owner.

English translation of the *Catechism of the Catholic Church* for the United States of America copyright © 1994, United States Catholic Conference, Inc.— Libreria Editrice Vaticana. Used with permission.

Other references cited as Notes at the end of each chapter.

© 2003 by Ave Maria Press, Inc.

All rights reserved. No part of this book may be used or reproduced in any manner whatsoever without written permission, except in the case of reviews and for pages explicitly designed to be used as part of the program.

International Standard Book Number: 0-87793-993-4

Cover and text design by Brian C. Conley

Printed and bound in the United States of America.

Library of Congress Cataloging-in-Publication Data
Lynch, Sean (Sean Michael)
          Tough choices : bringing moral issues home / Sean Lynch and Brian
O'Brien.
               p. cm.
          ISBN 0-87793-993-4 (pbk.)
     1. Christian ethics--Study and teaching (Secondary) 2. Christian
ethics--Catholic authors. I. O'Brien, Brian (Brian David) II. Title.

     BJ1249.L96 2003
     241'.042'0712--dc21

                                                                    2003007349

CONTENTS

To Our Families:
For always keeping the lines of communication open

INTRODUCTION
INTRODUCTION
INTRODUCTION
INTRODUCTION
INTRODUCTION
INTRODUCTION

INTRODUCTION

INTRODUCTION
INTRODUCTION
INTRODUCTION
INTRODUCTION
INTRODUCTION
INTRODUCTION
INTRODUCTION
INTRODUCTION
INTRODUCTION
INTRODUCTION
INTRODUCTION
INTRODUCTION
INTRODUCTION
INTRODUCTION
INTRODUCTION

Why *Tough Choices?* • • • • • • • • • • • • • • • •

The impetus of *Tough Choices* stems from four original goals.

In *Tough Choices*, students evaluate different courses of action to resolve moral dilemmas. They use their own reasoning but then also tap into viewpoints, experience, and logic of others whose opinions they value: namely, their parents. Often, children and adolescents are not aware of their parents' beliefs and are surprised by the resource they discover.

For example, one dilemma given as an assignment in this text and then discussed in class centered around a student attending a party without obtaining permission from parents. The student finds himself without a way home and surrounded by drunk friends. A large number of our students we knew were shocked to find out that their parents would much prefer they call home, get a ride from the parents, and deal with the punishment for breaking curfew rules later than ride home with someone who was drunk to avoid punishment. Although it seems to be the obvious solution, many of our students originally believed it would be best to take the risk of riding with a drunk driver. Yet through the familial communication, their perceptions changed. It is our hope that such interaction and sharing of beliefs have a positive influence on both students and parents. Therefore, the *first goal* of *Tough Choices* is to provide adolescents with a safe arena to explore difficult moral dilemmas with the help of those closest to them before they are forced to confront similar issues in their own lives.

The subject matter deliberated in these discussions is the focus of the *second goal*. Teens in today's society face moral dilemmas sooner, in greater complexity, and in increasing numbers than in any time in our past. Too often, children or adolescents need to make a choice between two equally legitimate possibilities or opportunities to arrive at a decision that could have a dramatic impact on the remainder of their lives. These decisions must sometimes be made on the spot, without time to evaluate the possible outcomes of their actions. Unfortunately, the only reasoning they have to rely on in these life-altering situations is their own. That is why *Tough Choices* centers around moral dilemmas. Not only are students forced to evaluate a situation that has many possible courses of action, they are required to do this hopefully *before* they actually have to face such situations in their own lives.

The second goal manifests itself in the discussion that takes place in the classroom after the completion of the *Tough Choices* assignment in the home. Ideally, classrooms should be small, self-contained communities. Part of what defines a community is the mutual sharing of ideas and values among its members. Therefore, the *third goal* of *Tough Choices* is to facilitate mutual respect and the sharing of ideas and values among class members through the medium of classroom discussion. As happens with the family, students are often surprised by their classmates' ideas. Many times, students feel as if they are the only ones to hold certain values, yet have discovered that they enjoy the same beliefs as many of their classmates. Furthermore, the environment of a *Tough Choices* discussion must be one of openness, where ideas are exchanged in an atmosphere of respect in order for students so see the many facets of each decision.

Because of the variance of beliefs on important ethical issues discussed in a classroom, much of the burden for fostering this second goal and helping to shape the complexities of any argument falls to the teacher. Teachers must have set guidelines for discussion. Teachers must allow the students to express themselves in an open forum. But teachers also need to help lead students toward decisions that will have a positive impact on their lives. And because this book is particularly meant to assist those students in Catholic schools, the Catholic school teacher has a pastoral responsibility to enunciate the Church's stance on a moral issue. However, teachers are very different in their beliefs, experiences, and education. What might be a familiar topic to one teacher might be extremely foreign to another.

The potential problem with *Tough Choices* is that the facilitator might be no more knowledgeable on a particular topic than the students themselves. Such situations could lead to uninformed or incomplete discussions, or even worse, discussions that help to convince students of a course of action that may prove detrimental to their lives. This uncertainty in regards to the facilitation of discussions led us to our *third goal*, to provide facilitators with concrete information surrounding subject matter for each moral dilemma presented. While we cannot ensure that the information will be used, we have attempted to at least provide the facilitator with background information that will make the individual factually consistent and competent enough to be able to facilitate a discussion.

The information provided as a supplement to the dilemmas in the first eleven subject areas can be divided into two sections: 1) issues surrounding the moral dilemma and, 2) the Catholic Church's teachings on the moral dilemma. In our own classrooms, we have discovered that sometimes our knowledge base has been inadequate on a particular subject. In those situations, we have wished that we had more information. By articulating the issues and arguments surrounding each subject, we hope that similar confusion can be avoided. The inclusion of secular topics that surround the issue provide the teacher with a well-rounded knowledge reserve from which to draw to enrich the discussion for the students. The stance of the Catholic Church has been added for the teachers' clarification and to help students realize the value of the principles espoused by the school which they attend.

We have observed a general trend in our society towards immorality. The pop culture in which we live, as demonstrated through the entertainment media and other socio-political mores, permits and promotes self-seeking behavior. Satisfying one's own needs has become the paramount objective in life. There is no longer the impetus to evaluate how our actions affect others, even ourselves in the long run. It seems as though we no longer share the same ethical norms, collective ideals, or societal values as past generations.

We believe the main contributor to this phenomenon is the breakdown of the family. All of us are aware of the usual symptoms of this epidemic, families where one or both parents is absent, the rise in time spent in the workplace, and the results, namely teen pregnancy, abortion, alcohol and drug abuse, and suicide. However, the problem lies deeper than the superficial, or often-quoted statistics.

In their twenty-six-part column in *Meridian Magazine*, "Re-valuing the Family," Richard and Linda Eyre highlight research explaining the growth of this dilemma.[1] Some of the most poignant facts include:

- Parents in the 1990s spent 40 percent less time interacting with their children than parents in the 1950s. This variance equals 10–12 fewer hours per week.
- Adolescents spend an average of three minutes a day alone with their fathers. Fifty percent of that time is spent watching TV.
- Twenty-eight percent of school-age children have at least one parent at home on a full-time basis—down from 57 percent in 1970.

These statistics demonstrate that the lack of both communication and family interaction contribute heavily to fracturing the family of the twenty-first century. No longer can we assume that parents/guardians sit down with their children to discuss "current events" or, more importantly, issues in each other's lives. The *fourth goal*—really the main goal of *Tough Choices*—is to encourage and facilitate discussion between family members.

While in the process of preparing this book, an *additional goal* became apparent, centering on the fact that many Catholics have a limited knowledge and understanding of Church doctrine.

Let us first frame the context. While teaching in Baton Rouge, Sean's senior religion class explored a variety of pressing theological issues that faced students in society today. One day, a local priest was invited to the school to speak about vocations and answer any questions the students might have. Sean encouraged his students to bring up anything that was on their minds and to which they did not have an answer. Not long after his class's session with the priest began, the question on everyone's mind was brought up: "When is the Church going to stop living in the past with regards to sexuality and sex?"

It was a question that many teens (and some adults) have on their mind. It is one that deserved an accurate answer. The priest's response that day resonated not only because of its simplicity and poignancy, but because of its effect on the students' attitudes. He said,

> I get this question a lot. And it's amusing to me because it reveals a difference in perception that a lot of people have. Let me put it to you this way. If more people are being killed in car accidents due to speeding than ever before, what should be done about it? According to the people who disagree with how the Church remains steadfast in its beliefs in modern times, the answer should be to raise the speed limit so that technically there is no longer any speeding. But this doesn't make sense because you would still have the same problems.
> No, the solution is for people to take greater caution when driving and obey the rules that were constructed for their benefit. Similarly, the problems of our society today do not stem from the Church's refusal to change its teachings, they stem from people's refusal to follow the wisdom of the Church. Think about it. If people truly followed what the Catholic Church calls them to do, problems like STDs, unwed teen pregnancy, abortion, and many other social dilemmas would never exist.

The reaction on the faces of the students was unforgettable. A light bulb seemed to go on in their heads. They finally understood why the Catholic Church calls us to act in the manner that it does. It is this explanation of a foreign concept that was missing in the students' minds, not the students' ability to accept the teaching. They want to accept, they want to believe, but they also want someone to give them the reason *why* they should believe and *why* they should live Catholicism.

Unfortunately, most Catholics today do not have anyone to explain the rationale behind many Church teachings. Both of us have been fortunate. We both came from loving Catholic families who put us through Catholic schooling. Then we were blessed enough to study at Catholic universities, Boston College and the University of Notre Dame, that challenged us to discover the meaning behind the doctrine and the rationale behind the teaching. Most Catholics do not enjoy a similar guiding environment that encourages and helps resolve spiritual examination and clarification.

Therefore, the final goal of *Tough Choices* centers around religious education. Since most Catholics know the rules, guidelines, and dogmatic particularities, this is not a book on catechetical instruction. However, it attempts to answer the question of *why* we, as Catholics, believe what we do regarding difficult moral issues. An increase in dialogue leads to an increase in understanding. An increase in *informed* dialogue leads to the formation of long-term personal beliefs.

How to Implement *Tough Choices* • • • • • • • •

There are several different methods by which *Tough Choices* can be implemented in the classroom. Whichever method is used, it should follow the same general outline:

1. Teacher assigns dilemma for students to take home

2. Student discusses dilemmas with parent

3. Student brings signed copy of the dilemma to school for class discussion

Keys to successful integration of this endeavor are the teachers and the parents. Both must be willing and able to invest in facilitation, candor, disclosure, and preparation. Parents should expect to be informed during the entire process. Each teacher should have set guidelines and deadlines which allow parent flexibility.

As previously mentioned, this book contains additional information for eleven types of moral dilemmas. The two types of information, secular issues and answers to common questions about the subject matter and the specific Catholic Church position and related Church doctrine, offer the facilitator a pre-structured knowledge base from which to lead and direct the discussion. Efforts should be made to familiarize yourself with the material before attempting to lead or facilitate a discussion. Also, it would be helpful to have on hand a copy of the *Catechism of the Catholic Church* and a bible as a reference tool.

The next sections describe eight different formats of *Tough Choices* implementation. A variety of methods are included to assure maximum teacher flexibility.

Method #1—*Tough Choices* as a Weekly Assignment

In this method, *Tough Choices* is distributed weekly. For example, *Tough Choices* would be distributed every Friday, and would be due the next Friday. On the due date, a teacher might set aside 15 to 30 minutes of class time for class discussion and group processing. Teachers could pick current issues that interest students, choose dilemmas randomly, or tie the *Tough Choices* in with lesson plans. Examples:

- *Tough Choices* lessons about abortion during a unit on human dignity.
- *Tough Choices* lessons about wealth/economic injustice during a unit on consumerism.
- *Tough Choices* lessons about shoplifting in a unit about the Ten Commandments.

This method has been used for the past few years in schools throughout the southern part of the United States, which were served by the University of Notre Dame's Alliance for Catholic Education. Parents and students have been consistent in having a positive evaluation of the program. Success with this method hinges on students completing the assignment at home with the parents, parental signature, and fostering an all-encompassing class discussion.

Method #2—*Tough Choices* as an Introduction to a Unit

A teacher can initiate a new unit or lesson plan by having students take home materials on a topic to be discussed. Within a given time frame, students return with the homework assignment to class to discuss. This allows the teacher to tailor class material to that class's particular needs. The parents are aware of what is being studied in class and can communicate concerns to teachers and students. Example:

> Unit Title: Respect Life (Human Dignity)—A *Tough Choices* dilemma about a new student
> in school who other students pick on would be appropriate.

The students are introduced to the unit theme and directed as the topic is integrated into the unit framework. The students can identify the rationale, and indeed the need to respect each person no matter who they are or what they look like.

Method #3: *Tough Choices* as One Activity within a Larger Unit

In addition to beginning a unit, *Tough Choices* can be one of the many tools a teacher uses *during* a unit. Along with reading, research projects, and tests, *Tough Choices* can be used to vary a teacher's approach to the subject with the added benefit of parent involvement.

Method #4: *Tough Choices* to Address a Classroom Problem

This method can be used as a proactive or reactive response to a particular classroom issue. Issues can range from a recurring classroom problem to a one-time school event. Examples:

- You are aware of rampant cheating in your school or classroom. You could send home a dilemma about cheating (tailoring it to the individual school) thus provoking a class discussion while allowing the teacher to reaffirm tacit guidelines after the students opinions have been heard and acknowledged.
- Students in your school are continually harassed by others. You could send home *Tough Choices* on school violence so that students would know what their parents think of these types of actions.
- A few weeks before prom or homecoming, a teacher could send home a *Tough Choices* about drinking and driving, underage drinking, pre-marital sex, rowdy behavior, or eating disorders.

Method #5— *Tough Choices* for Exclusively Boys or Exclusively Girls

There are issues which may need to be divided by gender. There may be issues that a teacher would like to bring up in a *Tough Choices* segment, but specifically for either boys or girls. *Tough Choices* offers that flexibility. Examples:

- Boys dilemmas: steroids/sexual harassment
- Girls dilemmas: body image/breast implants/rape

Method #6— *Tough Choices* Tailored for Individual Students

This method requires added flexibility and responsiveness by the teacher. *Tough Choices* can be tailored and assigned to one student based on the needs of a particular student. Assessment can take the form of parent/teacher, or student written response based on parent discussion. This method could take the place of a punishment thus turning negative actions into "teachable moments". Example:

> If a student in class has been caught cheating, a teacher could assign *Tough Choices* to that student only and not allow a re-test until *Tough Choices* is completed.

Be careful not to use *Tough Choices* in conjunction with punishment. Such a situation may make *Tough Choices* appear to be punitive and disciplinary instead of as a tool to foster family communication and idea generation.

Method #7— *Tough Choices* with Catholic Church Teachings

While *Tough Choices* is designed to increase moral development, it can be designed with specific Catholic teachings in mind. This can be beneficial for students and parents alike, as parents are often unaware of Church teaching in some areas. This will most likely be implemented in a religion class but the possibility for implementation can occur in any course in a Catholic school. Before implementing this method, the *Catechism of the Catholic Church* should be consulted. Examples:

- *Tough Choices* about respecting human dignity (abortion, death penalty, euthanasia, bullying) would correlate specific language from the *Catechism* for purposes of discussion. Questions and follow-up activities could then center around Church teaching.
- During a unit on World War II, a teacher could assign a *Tough Choices* about the Church's official teaching about war.

Method #8—*Tough Choices* in Elementary School

A popular method of character development in elementary schools is often known as "The Virtue of the Week". The classroom teacher, or the school as a whole, picks one characteristic of a moral person (examples: courage, honesty, self-control) and design activities around that virtue. *Tough Choices* could play a role in classrooms such as these. By sending home moral dilemmas (in simplified format for age-appropriate use), teachers involve parents in the classroom while encouraging the parental role of primary educators for their children. Teachers at the elementary level must design *Tough Choices* that are developmentally appropriate.

FAQs Concerning Implementation of *Tough Choices* • • •

- **Should I require a grade for the assignments?**

Yes! Students need motivation to sit down and initiate discussion on difficult issues. This may not be something that is routine in many households. A developmental hallmark of adolescence is independence from parental oversight, so sharing ideas on matters of faith and morals may not only be foreign, but may cause initial familial discomfort. While students may be reluctant at first, as the program continues, they will discover the value of dialogue with their parents. *Tough Choices* need not be a major part of the grade but rather enough to reflect the value of this component of their work. Initially, the grade may compel compliance. In a few months, it will become an expectation.

Teachers should offer parents flexibility in the completion of assignments (e.g., give a few days to a week for assignment completion) and privacy if the parents seek it. While this has not been the case in the past implementation of *Tough Choices*, there is a possibility that a parent may not want the teacher to know the contents of a family discussion. This should be respected and the teacher should make other accommodations for this student. There are several ways to take grades on *Tough Choices*. Here are a few suggestions:

1) *Parent Signature* Students are required to get a parent's signature at the bottom of the page and return the sheet to class. This method is easy to grade but opens up the possibility of forgery. To combat forgery, a teacher can check suspicious signatures versus originals in the school's front office or signatures obtained by the teacher earlier in the year. A teacher could also make random phone calls home to parents to check the progress of *Tough Choices* discussions. Good parent communication about *Tough Choices* is essential to combating forgery and overall success. If implementing *Tough Choices* on a regular basis, it is best to prominently *number* each one and include the *due date* so a parent would notice if an assignment was missed or was late. A teacher could also supply one sheet where signatures are compiled and kept in students' notebooks until a specified turn-in date.

2) Tough Choices *with a writing assignment.* In addition to, or in lieu of a parent signature, a teacher could require students to write a paragraph or one page summary of their discussion. The students and parents may write a summary together. Students could also keep a *Tough Choices* notebook where all dilemmas, reflections, and summaries are kept. Notebooks could be turned in with a summary assignment (reflection paper), for example: "What did I learn from my parents?" or "What insights have I gained from parent/classroom discussion?" or "How can I take what I've learned and apply it to my life?"

3) *Class discussion.* In addition, or in lieu of the above suggestions, teachers can grade class discussion input. A teacher can grade on amount and quality of input and/or on listening skills. A cautionary note along with this suggestion: By grading class discussions, students may talk just to talk and not necessarily to say something of value. Teachers should take precautions in implementing this particular component of grading.

- **How should I notify and inform parents about *Tough Choices*?**
  Without parental involvement, *Tough Choices* does not exist. The program itself is designed to help enhance parenting and parent-child relationships. While communication between parent and teacher may vary by school protocol, teachers must be clear in their expectations of students and parents. A teacher might explain some tips for successful discussions between parent and child. For example:

- Find a quiet place.
- Invite other family members to join in the conversation
- Allow at least twenty minutes to discuss the dilemma.
- Ask each other lots of questions and feel free to explore other topics.
- Encourage contact between parent and teacher if an issue seems particularly distressing to the student.

Here are a few suggestions on how to notify and inform parents:

1) Parent letter/Policy letter. Many schools require a policy sheet outlining a teacher's grading and discipline policies. This avenue is perfect for informing parents about *Tough Choices*. A brief explanation noting the purpose and procedures will help parents understand program goals and expectations.

Example from one teacher's policy sheet:

What is Tough Choices?

Every Friday, each student will be assigned a Tough Choices *sheet. This is designed to foster dialogue between parents and students on a variety of modern day issues. The expectations for* Tough Choices *are simple:*

1. *Discuss the scenario with an adult member of the family for at least twenty minutes.*
2. *Have the adult and student sign the bottom confirming that they discussed it.*
3. *Bring the signed sheet to class to turn in.* Tough Choices *will be discussed in class each Friday. Expect a new assignment each Friday.*

2) Parent meeting/"Back to School Night"/Open House. In addition to a parent letter, planned parent nights can be a great way to inform parents. While this time should not be spent totally on *Tough Choices*, it is another opportunity for parents to hear about *Tough Choices* and ask any questions they may have. Handouts further explaining what *Tough Choices* is and what it does may be appropriate. This is also a good time to solicit ideas from parents about what topics they would like to discuss with their children through *Tough Choices*.

3) Phone calls. Phone calls are the best way to check up on a student's individual progress. Calling home will also cut back on forgeries and allow the teacher to hear real feedback from parents. Student feedback can easily be gauged in the classroom. Phone calls also allow teachers to better explain the program to parents who have further questions. Stressing your availability by phone or personal contact not only enhances communication, but validates the importance of this endeavor.

4) E-mail. Some parents may use e-mail as a primary means of communication. Teachers should respond and use this as an opportunity to further parental contact. Teachers could ask parents for their e-mail addresses and then notify parents through a list serve as to what topic is being discussed that week. This should not be a teacher's lone method of communication. However, e-mail also allows parents to communicate issues they may want discussed or potential complaints they have with the program. In addition, many parents travel in their jobs. This mode of communication will allow the absent parent to be part of the process.

5) Parent newsletter. Many teachers use newsletters to communicate with parents. Information about *Tough Choices* could be included in a weekly/monthly newsletter. If working with younger children, the dilemma for the week or month could be included in the newsletter, thus preventing students from losing it.

- ### *What do I do with this book?*

We strongly recommend tailoring each *Tough Choice* to your specific classroom. When implementing *Tough Choices*, it would be easiest to simply photocopy a dilemma from the book and hand it out. We recommend re-doing each dilemma to insure that names used in the dilemmas are not students in your class or school. Access to dilemmas is available on-line. Address an e-mail to ToughChoices@avemariapress.com. You will automatically receive an e-mail response that includes attachment files saved in both Rich Text File (rtf) and DOS Text File (txt) format, generic formats.

We have found that using names applicable to specific ethnic groups or geographic regions may help the discussions. You may also want to change the situation and/or write it in your own style. The included sample at the end of this Introduction is what one teacher adopted to his own style and format. Middle and elementary school teachers who use *Tough Choices* need to alter the language and be more selective in topics to explore. *Tough Choices* has been tested as low as eighth grade but it can work in the younger grades as well. For middle school, it may be beneficial to add multiple choice answers instead of students developing questions and answers on their own. Whether elementary, middle, or high school level courses, or because of regional variations, teachers should be cautious and assure that dilemmas are age appropriate.

Here are some other "Do's" and "Don'ts" of *Tough Choices*, which may be helpful in effective implementation of the program:

DO •

- communicate expectations to parents clearly and early
- attempt to link *Tough Choices* to your curriculum
- be consistent with distribution and return dates
- revise the issues presented to fit the class situation (age appropriateness, racial/ethnic breakdown, gender, identifiers)
- remind students and parents of due dates to insure full participation
- initial topics should be less controversial. Start with cheating or friendship instead of abortion or divorce. For many families, disclosure is a foreign concept, and beginning with emotionally charged topics may thwart your effort and sabotage your program
- incorporate Church teachings whenever possible
- prepare for class discussions by reading relevant Catholic Church teachings, thinking of potential conflicts or controversial questions, and preparing for the question, "Teacher, what do you think?"
- verify parental/student signatures
- call parents if *Tough Choices* assignments are not being returned
- ask students and parents for topic suggestions
- coordinate with other teachers in your school, so you are not sending home repeated dilemmas
- allow parent flexibility if they do not want to discuss the dilemma
- frame *Tough Choices* in a positive light as a way for parents and students to come together on common ground.

- encourage parents to acknowledge their child's opinion, but share their reasoning if opinions differ
- be ready for parent disagreement with some dilemmas and questions
- ask "What should you do?" before you ask "What would you do?"
- ask parents and students to evaluate *Tough Choices* at the end of the quarter/semester for improvement the next time
- give a grade for participating in *Tough Choices*
- give clear expectations of in-class discussion procedures
- disagree with students at appropriate times and make them explore issues on a deeper level

DON'T •

- simply photocopy and pass out *Tough Choices* as it appears in the book
- use names of students in your class in the dilemmas
- let a small number of students dominate class discussion
- say "Your parents are wrong," but provide students and parents with the correct Church teaching.

- *How do I run a good* **Tough Choices** *discussion?*

It is first essential that all students have completed the assignment. Students who have not completed the assignment will bring only their opinions and not the insight gained from parental discussion. Teachers must set firm guidelines about participation in discussions.

A successful discussion hinges on the teacher. Discussion is not lecture time nor is it a time for a few students to dominate the discussion. It is a time when ideas are explored by the whole class. Students will gain insight not only from what their own parents shared but also from classmates who make insights about the dilemma. In addition, students will learn the skill of maintaining their position in the face of disagreement. No student should be allowed to ridicule another student's input.

Leading class discussions can be tricky. Often the hardest part is getting started. To help this process, teachers may want to allow students to write or reflect first, then discuss. By allowing this type of reflection or pre-thinking, doing something with their thoughts, it will help students better organize and get ready to discuss. Some good discussion questions for any *Tough Choices* are:

- What should <u>name of person(s) in dilemma</u> do?
- What did your parents have to say about this dilemma?
- Why do you think your parents said what they did?
- If you were a parent, what would you tell your child?
- Did you and your parents agree or disagree on this dilemma?
- What did you disagree about? What did you agree about?
- What did you learn from what your parents had to say?
- What did you learn from what your classmates shared?
- What does the Church say? Why does the Church say that?
  Other discussion ideas:

  1. Some teachers have explored the idea of using Socratic method when having a *Tough Choices* discussion. For example, one of the most important rules of Socratic discussion is to follow the argument wherever it leads. While this idea has not been universally tried, it could be a worthwhile endeavor for the upper level student, a student in a gifted/talented program, or other students who have an appropriate level of scholastic maturity.

Numerous books and articles have also been written on the subject and should be consulted before attempting this form of discussion.

2. A teacher could direct discussions in small groups. This would be helpful in classes where students are uncomfortable sharing. Small groups could be facilitated by adults or teacher's aides, if possible. If there is one classroom teacher, a group secretary could be assigned to record the conversation and the major points made.

3. How the students are arranged in the classroom has different effects on the discussions. Putting all students in a circle is one such option. This will depend on classroom size. If putting students in a circle, the teacher should make sure all students can see each other and that no student is outside the circle.

4. The timing of *Tough Choices* discussion can vary. Some teachers choose to do it at the beginning of class and place a time limit on the discussion (15 to 30 minutes). In using this method, teachers should be clear about time expectations as students could try to extend the conversation to avoid moving on to new activities. Others have done it during the last part of class as a closing exercise. A disadvantage to this method would be that a good discussion could be cut off due to time constraints.

- **How can *Tough Choices* be used in other high school courses besides religion?**
  Here are some ideas:

Science

Science courses offer exciting opportunities to use *Tough Choices*. Teachers can address moral scientific issues like abortion, cloning, genetics, and the end of life. Science also offers the ability to discuss Church teachings which go along these controversial issues. Dilemmas could also center around improperly using science in cloning, nuclear design, etc.

For both high school and middle school, topics including dissection, lab safety, animal testing, wildlife control, wearing fur or leather, genetically engineered food, and fetal tissue research could be tied into curriculum and involve parents. The teacher must review the science *and* morality for this type of discussion. It may be helpful to include an expert in these areas, such as a geneticist, biologist, or ethicist.

Math

This subject requires creativity. Similar to science, dilemmas could center around misusing math knowledge in the real world. An example may be cheating on your taxes or, as an accountant, "cooking the books" for the employer. Other dilemmas could center around misusing statistics and improper use of calculators and computers.

Social Studies

Social studies allows several avenues of very rich fodder. A teacher could design historical dilemmas around issues like race, gender, and immigration. Political dilemmas would be appropriate in a government or history class. An example could be about a United States senator who holds strong beliefs for gun control but whose constituents strongly oppose gun control. What should the senator do? United States history offers amazing opportunities to have students discuss dilemmas with parents and grandparents. Some examples could be: the role of women in society, the just war during World War II (the atomic bomb), draft dodging, civil rights, The Holocaust, European and American imperialism, child labor, and population control. Government and civics classes could center dilemmas around issues like voter fraud, perjury, bombing civilians to achieve a military objective, negative campaigning, selling arms in exchange for hostages, and spying. Dilemmas could also be used to bring out issues of race, gender, sexual orientation, and age discrimination. This would be appropriate in almost any social studies classroom, especially sociology and history. A sociology course could also tackle the topics of school funding, death/dying, and wealth.

English

English dilemmas depend on the literature being explored. Some examples of literary works and possible *Tough Choices* topics that could go with them are:

To Kill a Mockingbird— racism, integrity in the legal profession, and discrimination

The Great Gatsby—wealth, "looks over substance," and economic injustice

All Quiet on the Western Front—just war theory, violence, issues of conscience

The Diary of Anne Frank—discrimination, just war theory, a daily situation of standing by while another student is teased

The Color Purple – ethnic stereotype, rape, incest

Poetry of Langston Hughes—Racism, discrimination, treating others differently

Journalism—Breaking a scandalous story/ethics of reporting

Foreign Languages

Students could be given dilemmas in the foreign language and have to translate them to discuss at home with their parents. Dilemmas could include vocabulary words or verb tenses being covered in class all while addressing the moral dimension. *Tough Choices* could also center around racism, economic injustice, or overall issues of difference when relating language to a particular culture.

Computers

Tough Choices could center around the misuse of computers for hacking, internet pornography, burning CDs, violent video games, chat rooms, privacy violations, virus production, misusing another's screen name, internet plagiarism, and ruining people financially by fraud, deception, and computer theft.

Old Testament

Mr. Thompson

Tough Choices **#7 – due Friday, December 6th, 2002**

EATING DISORDER DILEMMA #1

Jill and Stacey have been good friends throughout high school. After Christmas break, they both decide to diet and exercise. They begin to watch what they eat and work out together. By the end of February, both girls are excited to see the results. Over the next month however, Jill notices that Stacey keeps getting thinner. Jill doesn't think much of this at first, but she begins to notice little things, such as Stacey throwing away her lunch and increasing her workouts to two hours a day. Jill becomes concerned and asks Stacey if maybe she is losing too much weight. Stacey laughs her off and tells Jill not to worry, that she is "only getting in shape for prom." A few weeks before prom, Jill notices how Stacey's clothes seem to hang on her and that Stacey seems much more withdrawn than usual. Jill again brings up the issue of weight loss, but Stacey gets angry saying, "I thought you were my friend." When Jill says she feels Stacey might need to talk to somebody about this, Stacey insists that such a move would ultimately end their friendship. Jill isn't sure if Stacey is anorexic or not. She is worried about losing her as a friend.

Discussion Questions:

1) What should Jill do?

2) What does "being a good friend" mean?

3) Is having a friend be angry with you sometimes okay?

4) To whom can Jill turn for help?

We have discussed this Tough Choice.

_____   _____

Parent/Guardian Signature   Student Signature

Notes

1. Richard Eyre and Linda Eyre. "Re-valuing the Family, Part Six: The Crisis That Exists for Families Today" *Meridian Magazine*, September, 2001. Found at: http://meridianmagazine.com/parentsjournal/001103revaluing6.html

ABORTION
ABORTION
ABORTION
ABORTION
ABORTION
ABORTION

ABORTION

ABORTION
ABORTION
ABORTION
ABORTION
ABORTION
ABORTION
ABORTION
ABORTION
ABORTION
ABORTION
ABORTION
ABORTION
ABORTION
ABORTION
ABORTION
ABORTION

Overview of Abortion Issues • • • • • • • • •

- **What is abortion?**

Abortion describes any voluntary termination, or the deliberate procedure that causes the termination, of an embryo or fetus before the embryo or fetus is sufficiently developed to survive on its own.

- **What is an embryo? What is a fetus?**

An embryo is a human being in its earliest stage of development, from the moment of conception until the eighth week of development. A fetus is the name for an unborn human from the eighth week of development until birth.

- **Is an embryo alive? Is a fetus alive?**

Yes. From the moment of conception, an embryo is a human being. Evidence of this is displayed in the development of the embryo/fetus that takes place inside the mother's womb.

Stages of Embryonic Development[1]

Day 1: Conception occurs, where the father's sperm penetrates the mother's egg cell. Genetic information from both parents interact to begin to create a new individual. Cell division begins (the first cell divides into two, the two into four, etc.). Size of the embryo is no bigger than a grain of sugar.

Days 5 to 9: The tiny human attaches itself to the wall of the mother's uterus.

Days 10 to 14: The mother's menstrual period stops due to a hormone produced by the child.

Day 18: The child's heart forms. Eyes begin to develop.

Day 20: The brain, spinal cord, and nervous system form.

Days 21 to 24: The child's heart begins to pump its own blood through a separate closed circulatory system with its own blood type.

Day 28: Eye, ear, and respiratory system begin to form. Muscles develop along the future spine. The budding of arms and legs occur.

Day 30: The child has grown 10,000 times its original size to 6–7 mm (1/4") long.

Day 35: The mouth, ears, and nose take shape. Pituitary gland in brain forms.

Days 42 to 43: Skeleton is formed. Brain waves coordinate movement of muscles and organs. Reflexes present. The penis begins to form in boys.

Day 45: Spontaneous movements have begun. Buds of milk teeth have appeared.

8 Weeks: All body systems and organs are present. Stomach produces digestive juices. Liver makes blood cells. Kidneys begin to function. Taste buds are forming. Child is 3 cm (1 1/8") long.

9 Weeks: Child squints, swallows, moves tongue, and makes fists. Thumb-sucking occurs. Fingernails begin to form. Fingerprints are visible.

11 Weeks: All body systems are working. Baby urinates, has spontaneous breathing movements, and makes complex facial expressions.

12 Weeks: The child can kick, turn, curl toes, move thumbs, bend wrists, turn head, open mouth. The child weighs one ounce.

16 Weeks: Genital organs clearly differentiated. Child swims and turns somersaults.

18 Weeks: The vocal chords work; the child can cry.

5 Months: The mother first feels baby's movements. Hair develops on the child's head. The baby weighs one pound and is 12 inches long.

7 Months: Teeth are present. Eyelids open and close while eyes look around. Hands grip

strongly. Mother's voice is heard and recognized.

8 Months: Baby weighs over two pounds and space in uterus gets cramped.

9 Months: The child triggers labor and birth occurs, usually 255–275 days after conception.

- **What are the types/methods of abortion?**
  Typically, abortions are divided into categories based on when the abortion procedure is performed.

Methods of early abortion include:[2]

Mifepristone (5 to 7 weeks). Also known as RU-486, this drug causes an abortion by interfering with the function of the placenta, starving the unborn child. The chemical also blocks the action of the hormone that makes the lining of the uterus hold onto the fertilized egg. The lining breaks down and the embryo is lost in the bleeding that follows. This method of abortion takes place over the span of several days. Usually, the woman will bleed heavily for between nine to twelve days, but some women have bled for four weeks. Long term health risks of mifepristone are not yet known.

Methotrexate (5 to 9 weeks). An injection of methotrexate kills the child by interfering with the cell division process. Several days later, a woman is treated with prostaglandin (explained later) suppositories to help expel the fetus, and the woman aborts at home. This method requires three doctor visits to complete the process.

Vacuum Curettage/Aspiration or *D&C* (6 to 16 weeks). Also called surgical suction, vacuum aspiration involves no cutting. After a local anesthetic is administered, a powerful suction tube is inserted into the uterus. The unborn child is torn apart by the force of the suction and the fetal body parts and placenta are sucked into a jar. Possible complications include infection, cervical laceration, and uterine perforation.

Methods of late abortion include:[3]

Surgical Dialation & Evacuation or *D&E* (15 to 20 weeks). A treatment that involves an overnight stay, this procedure also involves no cutting. Once a general anesthetic has been administered, the cervix is stretched open and the abortionist uses forceps to pull the child out of the womb, limb by limb. Similar complications of infection, cervical laceration, and uterine perforation can occur.

Prostaglandin (16 to 38 weeks). Also called misoprostol, this drug is injected or given as a suppository to induce a premature labor that is much like a miscarriage and which usually lasts six to twelve hours. Live births are common using this procedure. Bleeding lasts between five days and five months. Complications include convulsions, vomiting, and cardiac arrest.

Saline Abortion (16 to 32 weeks). This practice involves the insertion of a long needle into the woman's abdomen, where a salty solution is injected into the amniotic fluid. The salt burns the child's lungs and skin. The mother delivers a dead baby within 24 hours. Due to serious health risks to the woman, this method is infrequently used.

Digoxin Induction (20 to 32 weeks). A lethal chemical is injected into the baby's heart and labor is induced with prostaglandin.

Partial Birth Abortion or *D&X* (20 to 32 weeks). The baby is pulled out feet first while the head remains in the uterus. The abortionist then makes a hole in the back of the baby's skull and removes the brains with a suction catheter. This causes the head to collapse, allowing the dead child to be removed in one piece.

Hysterotomy (24 to 38 weeks). This procedure involves making an incision in the mother's abdomen, like a C-section. The baby is then removed and allowed to die from neglect.

- **How common are abortions? How many abortions are there?**

  According to the Alan Guttmacher Institute, which is a branch of Planned Parenthood that contacts hospitals and known abortionists, there are an estimated 1,550,000 abortions performed annually in the United States.[4] Compare that figure to the estimated 4,000,000 live annual births in the United States.

- **How do abortions affect mothers?**

  Some abortion proponents claim that abortions are actually safer than childbirth for the mother, but a closer look at the possible complications for the mother tells a different story.

  In 1985, the reported average maternal mortality from regular, live births was 4.7 per every 100,000 deliveries.[5] With the increase in technology and advance of medicine, that rate has dropped even lower, so that in developed nations, maternal mortality due to live births almost never occurs.

  Deaths of mothers due to complications stemming from abortions occur much more frequently. Keeping in mind that abortion injuries and deaths go unreported, the book, *Lime 5*, verified that in the year 1992–93, twenty-three mother deaths resulting from induced abortions were reported to state agencies.[6] This number does not take into account the many free-standing abortion clinic procedures or "back-alley" abortions that occur each day. But, of the women who die, the main causes of such deaths were infection, uterine perforation, hemorrhaging, viral hepatitis due to blood transfusions, pulmonary thromboembolism (blood clotting of the lungs), and disseminated intravascular coagulation (sudden drop in blood clotting ability resulting in internal bleeding and sometimes death) due to saline abortions.

  There are many nonlethal, physical side-effects, as well. Infection of the Fallopian tube, typically pelvic inflammatory disease (PID), can cause the tube to close shut on account of its tiny size and high fragility. PID can lead to infertility or chronic inflammation of the female reproductive organs. Young girls with immature cervixes can develop traumatic dilatation. A D&C procedure performed on a firmly closed uterus can cause a partially torn cervix or other cervical incompetence. Scar tissue can develop and complicate future pregnancies. Women who have had abortions are at a greater risk for mid-trimester pregnancy loss, premature delivery, and low birth weight babies for their pregnancies in the future.

  As damaging, if not more, are the psychological and social effects that plague women who undergo abortions. Dr. David C. Reardon, of the Elliot Institute, found that such women often experienced nightmares and flashbacks to the abortion procedure.[7] In their daily lives, these women typically suffered from high anxiety, feelings of guilt and fear, self-hatred, and hysterical outbreaks. The abortion procedure also affected their inter-personal relationships. Difficulty developing and maintaining personal relationships, trusting the man who made them pregnant, and ending the relationship with their partner were typical results of the abortion. Dr. Reardon found that these women were more likely to become self-destructive, experience dramatic personality changes, suffer nervous breakdowns, begin or increase the use of drugs, and think about or attempt suicide than women who did not undergo abortions. Thinking back on what abortion had done to their lives, 94 percent of the women surveyed admitted that they regretted having an abortion.

- **What is the legal status of abortions in the United States?**

  Originally, American laws forbade abortion. Interestingly, women were not punished for procuring abortions, only those who performed the procedures were subject to the laws.

  This began to change with the legalization of abortion in Colorado and California in 1967. This was followed three years later by the state of New York. No other state legislatures passed laws permitting abortions for any reason except to save the mother's life. However, these became a moot point when the Supreme Court handed down its 1973 decision, and imposed abortion as being legal in other situations as well. From that point on, abortion was legalized in all fifty states.

The history of Supreme Court cases dealing with abortion includes:

Griswald v. Connecticut, 1965 . A stepping stone to *Roe v. Wade*, this case made it unconstitutional to outlaw contraceptives of any kind. Griswald was the head of the Planned Parenthood League of Connecticut and she gave information, instruction, and other medical advice to married couples concerning birth control. She was arrested and convicted by a state law which made it illegal to counsel and provide other services to married people in an effort to prevent contraception. The state law was declared unconstitutional.

Roe v. Wade, 1973. This well-known case provided that abortions be legal, provided that there was a convincing reason to have one. In their opinion, the Supreme Court felt that the right to privacy was broad enough to include a woman's right to terminate her own pregnancy. It further then went on to say that embryos and fetuses were not persons because legal personhood can not exist prenatally, and therefore they are not covered by laws. Also, abortions for any reason would be allowed to be performed during the first three months of a woman's pregnancy. Lastly, abortions could be performed up until the moment of birth if a physician decided that it was necessary for the mother's health, be it socially, physically, emotionally, or psychologically.

Planned Parenthood v. Danforth, 1976. It ruled that it was unconstitutional to require a woman to receive spousal or parental consent before choosing to have an abortion. Also, it ruled that it was unconstitutional to prohibit saline abortions.

Belotti v. Baird, 1979. It cleared more barriers preventing minors from obtaining abortions. A Massachusetts law requiring minors to gain parental consent or seek a judge's permission should either of the parents refuse was struck down.

Colautti v. Franklin, 1979. It found that, in trying to determine when a baby can exist outside the womb, the issue of viability is up to the interpretation of the physician. Therefore, more women were able to get around restrictive rules regarding the latest time in their pregnancy that they were able to get an abortion.

Harris v. McRae, 1980. It declared that states are not required to pay for elective abortions for the poor.

City of Akron v. Akron Center for Reproductive Health, 1983. It determined that instituting mandatory waiting periods for women wishing to receive abortions was unconstitutional. Also, women did not need to provide informed consent. In other words, women did not have to demonstrate that they were knowledgeable about the procedure they were about to undergo. Also declared unconstitutional were laws requiring the "humane" disposal of the remains of the fetus and those imposing mandatory hospitalization of women for second trimester abortions.

Webster v. Reproductive Health Services, 1989. It required physicians in the state of Missouri who wished to perform an abortion to do a viability testing on any pre-born baby. It also put greater restrictions on the federal tax money that could be used to pay for abortions.

Hodgson v. Minnesota, 1990. It cleared some restrictions which had prevented minors from obtaining abortions. Under the Minnesota law, minors needed permission from both parents and a forty-eight hour waiting period before getting an abortion. The Court said that the notification of both parents did not serve a legitimate state interest and only one parent needed to be notified.

Planned Parenthood of Southeast Pennsylvania v. Casey, 1992. It reversed some of the Court's previous decisions by saying that some reasonable regulations on abortion could be adopted, including: parental notification if the female involved was a minor, requirements of informed consent, confidential reporting, and inclusion of a 24-hour waiting period. This allowed states to have the right to regulate how abortions are performed and to ban abortions after the fetus is viable (able to live outside the womb) unless the mother's life or health is endangered.

- **What are the main arguments *for* and *against* abortions?**
  1. The fetus is not human.

Argument: An unborn baby is not a person because it does not yet have the properties that make up a person. "Pro-choice" advocates point out that the brain does not function until forty days into the pregnancy. Since the main medical criterion for death is cessation of brain wave activity, then, the argument follows, the onset of brain wave activity constitutes the beginning of life. Therefore, abortions are allowable for a period of time during the pregnancy. Another version of this argument was used by the Supreme Court in *Roe v. Wade*. The Court admitted it did not know when life begins, but that did not prevent it from separating personhood from humanity. The justices reasoned that a developing fetus was a human, but not a person. Since only persons are given 14th Amendment protection under the Constitution, the Court argued that abortions could be legal at certain times.

A final take on this argument has to do with the issue of *viability*. Viability refers to the ability of the fetus to live, on its own, outside the womb. Abortion proponents argue that since a fetus is dependent on the mother for survival, it cannot live on its own and is therefore not a person.

Response: Medical technology has made this argument a moot point in the past few decades. Ultrasound equipment has enabled physicians to witness the development of the fetus throughout the gestation process. It is clear that the embryo develops human traits from the moment of conception (see Stages of Embryonic Development, page 20–21).

Also, at the moment of conception, the embryo is genetically different from the mother. To argue that the embryo is no different from a mother's appendix is medically inaccurate. While a sperm and egg each contain 23 chromosomes, a human being consists of 46 (and sometimes 47) chromosomes. There is a difference between the DNA of a mother and the DNA of an embryo.

The argument for viability is a weak proposition. Can a fetus live outside the mother and take care of itself? No, but neither can a one-year old baby. And if a one-year old baby cannot take care of itself, shouldn't it be considered less than human as well? To make one concession on the argument for viability allows dangerous conclusions to be made about human life in other areas.

In much the same way, the Supreme Court's distinction between being human and personhood walks a similar slippery slope. By choosing biological criteria to define "person", the Court allowed states to outlaw abortions performed after a child was viable. But since viability is an arbitrary criterion, there is no biological reason why there has to be a line drawn during the early stages of embryonic development. Using a vague distinction for personhood, it is a legitimate possibility that similar arguments could be made for infanticide and euthanasia.

2. The abortion question is a religious issue.

Argument: Due to our Constitutional rights as Americans, there is a separation between church and state. By passing laws outlawing abortions, the government imposes moral judgment on a secular issue. The abortion question should be debated by churches and philosophers, not legislators.

Response: Correct, abortion *is* a moral issue. But so is war, poverty, racism, and other societal evils that legislators address. In fact, all laws embrace a particular individual's morality while challenging another's. This does not mean that such topics are beyond the scope of our government. It simply highlights the human element that our country's lawmakers must use to create laws.

3. Abortions are better than giving birth to unwanted children.

Argument: Because most mothers seeking abortion do not want the child they carry, pro-choice advocates state it is better that the child be aborted rather than grow up in a home knowing it is unplanned, unwanted, and/or unloved.

Response: How can one possibly measure the value of a life never experienced? There is no value in not existing, but all life has value in and of itself, regardless of the perceived lack of quality assigned to it by the views of outsiders.

There are no studies that show that unwanted pregnancies increase the percentage of unwanted children as opposed to planned pregnancies. Also, some confusion exists between an "unplanned" and an "unwanted" pregnancy. If we think of the pregnancies of couples that we know, was each pregnancy planned or was it a surprise? (And in all honesty, is every couple initially happy when they find out they are pregnant?) Many women and couples experience much joy from pregnancies they initially did not plan.

Legalizing abortion has not reduced child abuse. It simply has added to the notion that "unwanted" children have less value than children who are "wanted".

We set a dangerous precedent when we assume that any level of being "planned" or "wanted" determines the value of life. Acts of genocide throughout our world's history demonstrate the danger of relating the two concepts.

Lastly, how can anyone claim that a child is "unwanted" given the prevalence of couples waiting to adopt a child? Some couples stay on waiting lists for years before they have the opportunity to adopt a child of their own. There is a greater demand of couples wanting to adopt than there is a supply of "unwanted" children being born.

4. Unwanted children have higher incidence of violence later in life.

Argument: Unwanted children who are neglected or battered often become criminals later in life. The fact that a mother did not want the child means that there will be a continual pattern of disdain expressed towards the child, whether passively or actively.

Response: No studies prove that unwanted pregnancies lead to higher instances of battered children. On the contrary, a 1980 study of battered children done at the University of Southern California by Professor Edward Lenoski revealed that 91 percent of the 674 battered children in his study were planned and wanted, compared to the 63 percent in national control populations.[8]

Also, there is no definitive connection between unwanted pregnancies and criminal behavior. Sure, studies have shown a relation between battered children and criminal behavior, but the same connection does not hold true for unwanted pregnancies. To argue for abortion for this reason simply neglects our calling to love these unwanted children. Also, to insinuate that anyone can predict the outcome of human life from something as simple as whether or not a pregnancy is planned is ridiculous.

A counter-argument could be that aborted children never get the chance to become lawyers, poets, teachers, or loving parents. Many criminals have an opportunity to change their lives to become productive members of society. Should we do less for our developing fetuses?

5. There is overpopulation in the world.

Argument: With the birth rate increasing and death rate decreasing, the fixed amount of land and food resources on earth means that the globe is becoming overpopulated. *U.S. News & World Report* found that people born in the United States in 1970 had a life expectancy of seventy years. In 1993, it was seventy-six years. By 2050 it will be eighty-two years.[9] Couple this with the shortage of food availability that was described by Paul Ehrlich in his 1968 book, *Population Bomb*, and you come up with a real problem. Abortion would provide an easy answer to the difficult question of overpopulation and food shortage.

Response: It is true, people are living longer lives due to modern medicine and technology. But there is no problem with either overpopulation or food shortages. Yes, there are more people on the earth than ever before, but the problem is not with overpopulation, but with over-concentration of individuals in certain places. There are plenty of areas to live which have not yet been fully colonized. Also, according to the *New York Times & Gannett*, the world's food production has grown much more rapidly in the past few decades than the number of people.[10] A 1994 report conducted by the Council for Agriculture Science & Technology, explains how even if the earth's population were to double to 10 billion people, everyone could still have enough space to live and enough food to eat.[11]

6. Abortion is a woman's right to privacy and control over her own body.

Argument: Since the fetus is not human, is not viable and is dependent on the mother's body for survival, it is up to the mother to decide what she wants to do with her pregnancy and with her body. This is part of the mother's "freedom of choice", which is a natural right of hers.

Response: The right to control one's body is not absolute. It does not allow an individual to infringe upon the rights of other individuals. Therefore, it does not override the fundamental right to life enjoyed by all persons. It is not a private issue either, due to the potential of the unborn child to affect society, or the ways in which abortions affect the interpersonal relationships of the mother.

"Freedom of choice" is not guaranteed by our Constitution. The pregnant mother already exercised her freedom of choice when she chose to have sexual intercourse.

7. Abortions should be legal so that cases of rape and incest are taken into account, or in the event that a woman's life is threatened by pregnancy or childbirth.

Argument: Abortions are horrible, but outlawing them means that there is no option for women whom are the victims of rape or incest. Furthermore, such action would forbid performing an abortion to save a mother's life should complications arise during childbirth.

Response: While this argument is stronger than some of the others, it reveals an educational deficit of the people who make this claim. According to the Justice Department's 1995 *National Crime Victim Report*, of the 170,000 completed rapes and 140,000 attempted rapes each year, only about 170–340 result in pregnancies, or about one to two out of every thousand.[12] So the occurrence of such a phenomenon is very rare. But that being the case, there is still the option for women who are pregnant due to being the victims of rape to put their child up for adoption should they not want it. Also, the rape is not the fault of the child. Killing an innocent baby for the crimes of the father does not define justice.

Due to significant advances in obstetric and pediatric medicine, the situations which require killing the child to save the mother's life are extremely rare. When two lives are threatened and only one can be saved, physicians must always save that life.

8. Making abortions illegal will cause thousands of women to die, due to "back alley" abortions.

Argument: Outlawing abortions will increase the number of women who seek "illegal" abortions in procedures conducted by unauthorized personnel.

Response: Many abortion advocates admit their claims that thousands of women died from illegal abortions were made up in order to derive support for their case in the year leading up to *Roe v. Wade*.

In the year of that famous case, there were 39 deaths in the United States due to illegal abortions.[13] While this is a tragedy, the willful killing of 1.55 million babies each year through abortions is not the answer. Women must be made aware of opportunities available to help them and their babies live healthy lives.

National Helplines

Counseling

Bethany Christian Services: 1-800-BETHANY

Post–Abortion Counseling

Rachel's Vineyard: 1-877-HOPE-4-ME or 1-800-5-WE-CARE

24 Hour Pregnancy Hotlines

Birthright: 1-800-550-4900

National Life Center: 1-800-848-LOVE

Hotlines offering Referrals

Birthright: 1-800-550-4900

The National Crisis Pregnancy Hotline: 1-800-852-5683

Catholic Charities: 1-800-CARE-002

The Nurturing Network: 1-800-TNN-4MOM

Adoption Information

Bethany Christian Services: 1-800-BETHANY

Church Teaching on Abortion • • • • • • • • •

- **What is the Catholic Church's position on abortion?**
  The Catholic Church is unequivocally against the practice of abortion. This has been Church teaching since the first century. It "has not changed and remains unchangeable" (*CCC*, 2271). The teaching is best summarized in paragraph 2270 of the *Catechism of the Catholic Church*::

  > Human life must be respected and protected absolutely from the moment of conception. From the first moment of his existence, a human being must be recognized as having the rights of a person—among which is the inviolable right of every innocent being to life.

- **Why is that the position of the Catholic Church?**
  The Church believes that all human life begins at conception. Because life begins at conception, abortion is the killing of a human life. This is true at all stages of pregnancy. The Catholic Church holds that abortion does "irreparable harm" to the developing fetus for whom life is terminated, the parents of the child, and "the whole of society." Therefore, abortion is not just "a decision between a woman and her doctor" as is often said. It *is* the taking of a human life.

- **Which Scripture passages are relevant to the abortion issue?**
  Old Testament

  Psalm 22:10–11

  Psalm 139:14–15

  Ecclesiastes 11:5

  Sirach 49:7

  Isaiah 44:2

  Isaiah 44:24

  Isaiah 49:1

  Isaiah 49:5

  Jeremiah 1:5

  New Testament

  Luke 1:39–44

- **What else should I know about abortion?**
  1. Recently, new technology exists which can cause premature termination of fetal life. A current debate surrounds the drug, RU-486, often referred to as "the morning after pill." This medication alters the lining of the wall of the mother's uterus, thus preventing implantation of the fertilized ovum, already a human, seven to ten days after conception. The Catholic Church views this as another means to abort a developing baby and therefore immoral.
  2. Cooperating with anyone who chooses to abort a baby is a "grave offense." This would include health care professionals who participate in the act of abortion. For a friend of someone who wishes to obtain an abortion, it is important to note that any cooperation is a "grave offense" in other words, immoral. Helping a friend who is pregnant should

mean helping her realize that she carries human life. A true friend finds ways to support her in carrying the baby to term.

3. Abortion in the cases of rape and incest still terminates a human life. The Church is opposed to abortion even in these terrible circumstances. The baby is a gift from God and the circumstances under which that baby was conceived do not outweigh that baby's right to life.

4. As previously discussed, when the mother's life is in danger, every effort must be made to save both. When speaking of "the mother's life in danger", many contemporary arguments in favor of abortion include a women's mental health or future convenience. Exceptions for the life of the mother means the mother will physically die if she gives birth. As noted earlier, these instances are very rare, but do occur.

5. Because life begins at conception, the Church prohibits using human embryos for the purpose of research. Human life begins at conception which means these human embryos are in fact human beings.

- **What should I do to help stop abortion?**
  Numerous opportunities exist to stop the tragedy of abortion including:

  1. Become politically involved to help change the laws regarding abortion. The *Catechism of the Catholic Church* states that "the inalienable rights of the person must be recognized and respected by civil society and the political authority" (2273).
  2. Publicly protest the practice of abortion. Contact your local Right to Life group. The National March for Life takes place in Washington, D.C. on January 22 every year.
  3. Participate in or start a Pro-life club at your school or in your church.
  4. Be sure the money you spend is not used to support organizations that promote abortion.

ABORTION DILEMMA #1

Laura and Jeannie have been good friends for ten years. One weekend Laura was at a party and had too much to drink. At the end of the night she had sexual intercourse with a classmate. Three weeks later Laura told Jeannie that she is pregnant. Laura is scared, confused, and is not sure what she wants to do. Laura mentions that she is thinking of having an abortion and she doesn't want to tell her parents. She tells Jeannie not to mention it to anyone.

Discussion Questions:

1) What should Laura do?

2) Should it matter that Laura was drunk when she became pregnant?

3) What should Jeannie do?

4) In this situation, what does being a friend mean?

We have discussed this Tough Choice.

_____   _____

Parent/Guardian Signature   Student Signature

ABORTION DILEMMA #2

Kyle and Liz have been best friends since they were eight years old. Mostly because of the length and depth of their friendship, there has never been any physical attraction between Kyle and Liz. In fact, they each steadily dated others. But there was no doubt about how the two cared for each other.

Liz had found out three weeks ago that she was pregnant. Kyle was the first and only person she told. She had already made up her mind to have an abortion, but she needed to hear from Kyle that he would still like her and respect her. Kyle did not know what to think or do. He personally abhorred abortion, and had always taken pro-life stands in any discussion or debate. This attitude was a result of influence from his parents, who were also vocally pro-life and attended protests at some clinics.

Liz had already made the appointment at the clinic. Though she knew full well Kyle's beliefs, Liz nevertheless felt that their friendship should outweigh Kyle's personal convictions. She asked Kyle if he would take her to the clinic on the day of the abortion. This was the very clinic where Kyle had once marched in a peaceful abortion protest with his parents. He was conflicted because Liz was his best friend, and he could not imagine her having to go through this alone.

Discussion Questions:

1) What should Kyle do?

2) How should Kyle weight his beliefs versus his friendship?

3) Does he have to choose one over the other?

4) Should it matter that his parents are strongly against abortion?

We have discussed this Tough Choice.

_____   _____

Parent/Guardian Signature   Student Signature

ABORTION DILEMMA #3

Christy lives with her five children in a two-room apartment. She is only twenty-five years old. Though she has spent much of her life either using drugs or in rehab, she has recently finished her first year of sobriety. For the past year and a half she has worked as a waitress at a local diner. The money she makes isn't much, but it is enough to keep the heat turned on and her children fed and clothed. Christy hopes that if she provides for her children, they will finish school and make better lives for themselves.

Christy recently discovered she is pregnant again. She is terrified of the consequences. Her boyfriend (the father of her youngest daughter) refuses to see her or have anything to do with her. Christy knows that if she keeps her baby, it will mean one more mouth to feed. Also, the child would need constant care and supervision. Who would provide this? She can't afford to quit her job and her children are all too young to care for themselves. Giving the baby up for adoption would mean that she would have to take a month off of work and probably lose her job. In addition to all of this, one of the doctors at the free clinic down the street has warned Christy that it is possible that her baby may be born with some birth defects due to the damage done to her body through the years of drug use.

Christy is beginning to think that abortion may be her only option. She doesn't see any way to give birth to this baby and keep food on the table at the same time.

Discussion Questions:

1) What is the dilemma Christy faces?

2) Make a list of Christy's choices, and the possible positive and negative consequences of each of these choices.

3) What are options that Christy may have overlooked, or any additional means of support and assistance?

4) What moral decision do you think Christy should make? Why?

We have discussed this Tough Choice.

_____   _____

Parent/Guardian Signature   Student Signature

Notes

1. M. Allen et. al., "The Limits of Viability," *New England Journal of Medicine*. vol. 329, no. 22 (25 November 1993): 1597.

http://www.abortionfacts.com/literature/literature_921ms.asp

http://www.w-cpc.org/fetal.html

2. http://www.cpcworld.org/methods.html

http://www.btinternet.com/~DEvans_23/ab_meth.htm

3. Ibid.

4. Abortion Surveillance U.S. 1988 Morbidity & Mortality Weekly Report, Centers for Disease Control, Atlanta (July 1991) and S.K. Henshaw et al., "Abortion Services in the U.S., 1987–1988," *Family Planning Perspectives* 22, no. 3 (May–June 1990):103.

5. Council on Scientific Affairs, AMA "Induced Termination of Pregnancy...,"; *JAMA*, 268, no. 22 (9 December 1992): 3231.

6. M. Crutcher, "Cooking the Books" in *Lime 5: Exploited by Choice* (Genesis Pub) 135.

7. *The Post-Abortion Review*, 2 no. 3: (Fall 1994) Available from the Eliot Institute, P.O. Box 7348, Springfield, Illinois 62791-7348.

8. E. Lenoski, *Heartbeat*. 3, no. 4 (December 1980).

9. *U.S. News & World Report*, 14 August 1995, p. 9.

10. *New York Times & Gannett*, 24 October 1994

11. Council for Agricultural Science & Technology, *"How Much Land Can Ten Billion People Spare for Nature,"* 4420 Lincoln Way, Ames, Iowa 50014.

12. *National Crime Victim Report*, U.S. Justice Department, August 1995, R. Bachman, ed.

13. http://www.mdrtl.org/Arguments.html

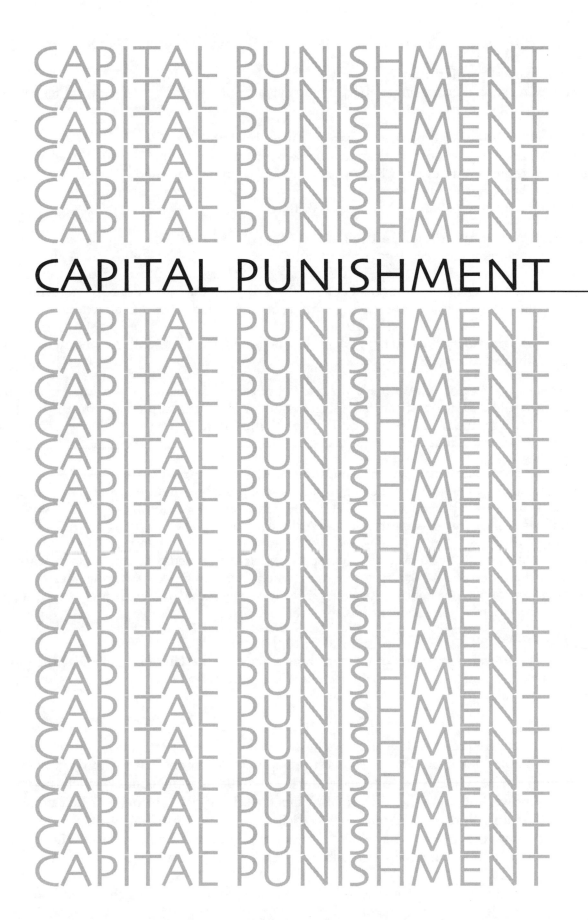

CAPITAL PUNISHMENT

Overview of Capital Punishment Issues • • • •

- **What is capital punishment?**

  Capital punishment is the imposition of the penalty of death by the state in response to the conviction of a certain crime.

- **What are the historical origins of capital punishment?**

  Accounts vary, but we know that capital punishment was practiced in ancient times, as evidence of its existence is found in the Code of Hammurabi (c.1750 B.C.). It continued to be practiced and widely applied throughout Western Europe and only met with societal resistance beginning in the eighteenth century with the writings of Montesquieu and Voltaire.[1]

- **Is capital punishment legal in the United States?**

  Capital punishment has been legal throughout the existence of the United States. However, due to the manner in which it was practiced, in 1972's *Furman v. Georgia*, the U.S. Supreme Court ruled that capital punishment was unconstitutional because it was applied disproportionately to certain classes of defendants, most often African-Americans and the poor. This decision voided all federal and state death penalty laws at the time but allowed for future ones to be created by Congress or state legislatures. The reasoning behind the ruling was that capital punishment violated the Eighth Amendment's "cruel and unusual punishment" clause.

  The 1976 *Gregg v. Georgia* case allowed the practice of capital punishment to resume in certain states. Currently, thirty-eight states and the federal government have reinstituted the death penalty.[2] Most death penalty laws are made at the state level, although the federal government does execute people for certain crimes against the federal government.

- **For what crimes can someone receive the penalty of capital punishment?**

  Most often, a person would only be eligible for capital punishment if he or she were found guilty of murder and were being charged in a federal court or in a state court located in a state with legalized capital punishment. However, according to the American Society of Criminology's Division on Critical Criminology, there have been 924 men executed for rape and 80 for attempted rape since 1800.[3] This does not include a crime of both murder and rape where it is assumed that murder is the capital crime. People can receive the death penalty for murder when that crime occurs during the commission of another, such as robbery or rape. A person can also be sentenced to death for treason against the government, especially when it puts at risk the lives its citizens.

- **What are the different types of capital punishment?**

  Today, there are five types of capital punishment used in the United States: electrocution, firing squad, gas chamber, hanging, and lethal injection. More explanation of each and the states where they are practiced are offered below.

  > *Electrocution*
  > Sometimes referred to as the "electric chair," the condemned person is led into a chamber containing the chair. The person is strapped to the chair and has electrodes fastened to his or her head and legs. Voltage courses through the condemned individual's body. It is not known how long the individual retains consciousness. It sometimes takes longer than the initial thirty second burst of electricity to kill the individual. States where electrocution is practiced: Alabama, Arkansas, Florida, Georgia, Indiana, Kentucky, Nebraska, Rhode Island, South Carolina, Tennessee, and Virginia.
  > *Firing Squad*
  > This method involves a condemned individual being strapped into a chair and hooded.

A target is placed on the prisoner's chest. Five marksmen are given bullets (one of them is given a blank), take aim, and fire. States where firing squad executions still are legal: Idaho and Utah.

Gas Chamber

In this method a condemned prisoner is strapped in a chair within a sealed chamber. There is a container directly underneath the prisoner. When the chamber door is sealed and the signal is given, the person in charge of the execution opens a valve releasing hydrochloric acid into this container. A second signal results in the release of approximately 8 ounces of potassium cyanide crystals or tablets into the acid, producing hydrocyanic gas, which destroys the ability of the blood hemoglobin to absorb oxygen. After the condemned individual inhales, it takes only a few seconds to lose consciousness. Death occurs within six to eighteen minutes. After pronouncement of death, the chamber is cleared through the use of carbon and neutralizing filters, and individuals in gasmasks decontaminate the body and chamber with a bleach solution. States which use the gas chamber: Arizona, California, Maryland, Mississippi, and North Carolina.

Hanging

The oldest form of execution, hanging involves a condemned individual stepping onto a raised platform, or the gallows. The person's neck is placed into a hoop, or noose, made at the end of a rope. The other end of the rope is secured above the gallows. On a signal the floor of the gallows gives way, and the individual is suspended by only the noose. This should break the individual's neck, although strangulation can also occur. States which administer death by hanging: Montana and Washington.

Lethal Injection

The most common of all forms of capital punishment, lethal injection has been used since 1982. In this method, the prisoner is secured to a gurney with ankle and wrist restraints. Cardiac monitor leads and a stethoscope are attached. An intravenous saline line is inserted into each arm, and the inmate is covered with a sheet. During the process, the prisoner will receive a dosage of three drugs. The saline lines are turned off and the first drug, sodium thiopental, is injected, putting the condemned into a deep sleep or causing unconsciousness. The second chemical, pancuronium bromide, is a muscle relaxant that stops respiration. Injection of the third drug, potassium chloride, stops the prisoner's heart. States which use lethal injection: Arizona, Arkansas, California, Colorado, Delaware, Idaho, Illinois, Kansas, Louisiana, Mississippi, Missouri, Montana, Nevada, New Hampshire, New Jersey, New Mexico, New York, North Carolina, Ohio, Oklahoma, Oregon, Pennsylvania, South Dakota, Texas, Utah, Virginia, Washington, and Wyoming. When the death penalty is applied to a federal criminal offense, the United States government uses lethal injection. Executions occur in Terre Haute, Indiana.

Twelve states do *not* have the death penalty: Alaska, Hawaii, Iowa, Maine, Massachusetts, Michigan, Minnesota, North Dakota, Rhode Island, Vermont, West Virginia, Wisconsin (also Washington D.C.).

- **May children or mentally challenged individuals ever be put to death in capital punishment cases?**

Typically, the cut-off age for possible execution is eighteen years old. Individuals also have to demonstrate various intellectual capacities to be deemed eligible for the death penalty. However, certain circumstances allow for convicted individuals below the age of eighteen or mentally challenged criminals to be put to death in a capital punishment crime. In *Thompson v. Oklahoma* (1988), the Supreme

Court ruled that the Constitution prohibits execution for crimes committed at age 15 or younger. However, in *Stanford v. Kentucky* (1989), the Court said capital punishment was permissible for crimes committed at ages 16 or older. A total of 221 juveniles have received death sentences since 1973, but only twenty-one of those have been executed.[4] Since 1977, thirty-three persons with mental retardation have been executed in capital punishment cases.[5] Until 2002, the federal government and the following states forbid execution of mentally challenged individuals: Arkansas, Colorado, Georgia, Indiana, Kansas, Kentucky, Maryland, Nebraska, New Mexico, New York, Tennessee, and Washington. In June 2002, the Supreme Court banned executions of the mentally retarded.

- ## What are the main arguments for and against capital punishment?
  1. Capital Punishment is a safe and painless means of executing a condemned individual.

Argument: The various forms of capital punishment do not violate the "cruel and unusual" provision in the 8th Amendment as laid out by our forefathers. "Cruel and unusual" were never defined at our nation's beginning, but the very fact the Supreme Court has upheld capital punishment's legality means that it does not violate the Constitution. Also, the forefathers never had to witness the rise in violent crimes that we have in our society today. It plays a key role in the protection of public welfare and safety.

The methods of capital punishment are not barbarous, but rather are the most humane means of exterminating a condemned individual's life. Hanging, firing squads, electrocution, gas chambers, and lethal injections all are quick and relatively pain-free ways to remove life from a person.

Capital punishment is not a case of "combating violence with violence." There is a difference between violence and law enforcement. Law enforcement may involve punishment. It is the end result of violence. Murder is the *unlawful* killing of an individual with malice and forethought. Capital punishment is not the same as murder, since the death penalty is the law. Those who commit violence and murder act outside the law, whereas those enforcing death penalty use the law.

Response: Capital punishment *is* cruel and barbarous. This thinking goes along with the constitutional prohibition of "cruel and unusual punishment". Proponents of this stance believe that capital punishment is a crude, ancient relic of older times, when institutions such as slavery, branding, and other corporal punishments were also widely accepted. It is designated to be unusual because the United States is the only industrialized western nation that continues to practice this punishment.

In much the same way it is seen as barbarous due to the methods by which it is administered. Numerous examples exist that point out extreme pain and suffering inflicted upon condemned individuals during the final execution of the death penalty. Hanging has resulted in slow, agonizing strangulation deaths or instances of heads being torn from the body. Electrocution often needs more than one periodic jolt of electricity, and witnesses have complained about the physical repulsion at seeing individuals jerk against their restraints and smelling burning flesh. Gas chambers often lead to violent convulsions for the condemned during the death struggle. Lethal injections, the most humane, allow no visible signs of pain or struggle due to the suppression of the central nervous system by drugs, but no factual studies have been done that prove pain is not being felt by the condemned.

2. Capital Punishment is an economically intelligent alternative to incarcerating a condemned individual to a life in prison at the taxpayers' expense.

Argument: The choice people have is between executing a convicted individual or having that individual drain taxpayer resources as they rot in a cell while serving a life sentence. For many of these condemned individuals, there is no opportunity for parole, so there is no chance that they will ever be released from prison. Executing an individual costs much less than providing for that individual for the rest of his or her life.

Response: The death penalty is not, nor ever has been, a more economical alternative to life in prison. This seems like an illogical statement, but in reality, it is the truth. A murder trial normally takes much longer when the death penalty is at issue than when it is not. A majority of the costs for this litigation is borne by the taxpayer. A 1989 Maryland study revealed that a death penalty case costs "approximately 42 percent more than a case resulting in a non-death sentence."[6] Two Texas counties estimated that the cost of a capital trial was between $400,000 and $600,000.[7] A similar non-capital murder trial costs about $75,000, or a difference of, on average, $425,000 to try each capital defendant. This does not take into account the appeals process mandated in death penalty cases. The same counties conservatively estimated that, due to the appeals process, only about 50 percent of all capital trials will result in an actual execution, therefore the actual cost of each execution would be $850,000. If that same amount was invested at a 5 percent rate of return, it would yield roughly $45,000 per year; more than enough to support someone serving a life sentence.[8]

Capital trials deal with the issue of time in relation to money. If a person were sentenced to life in prison, he or she could appeal, but that person would continue to serve his or her sentence in the meantime. But for a death sentence, serving the sentence would mean being executed, so the appeals process must take place in a shorter amount of time, which pushes back other court proceedings, resulting in increased losses of money and man-hours.

3. Capital punishment acts as a deterrent to future crimes.

Argument: The existence of the death penalty causes certain potential criminals to think twice about committing their crimes. Criminals are well-aware of the judicial system that is in place in our country. They know that being convicted of a crime, in the absence of the death penalty, means that they spend time in jail supplied with all their meals, education, and medical care while the appeals process will work to get them freed. They are aware that "life sentences" rarely, if ever, mean that they will be incarcerated for the rest of their lives. Therefore, they are fairly certain that, regardless of the outcome of their actions, they will live freely in the future.

However, if there *is* the possibility of the death penalty, criminals are faced with the ultimate decision before committing a crime. The possibility of having their lives taken may deter them from carrying out their plans. Even if the fear of capital punishment prevents one potential criminal from going through with their intended actions, then the existence of capital punishment will be justified.

Some statistics back up these claims. In 1977, Gary Gilmore faced a firing squad in Utah. There had been 55 murders in Utah during 1976. In 1977, in the wake of Gilmore's execution, there were only 44 murders, a 20 percent decrease.[9]

It has been mentioned that there was a temporary suspension of capital punishment in the United States from 1972–1976. Because of this the number of executions in the years immediately after the suspension were well below the numbers before it. However, the number of murders increased. In 1960, there were 56 executions and 9,140 murders. In 1964, there were only 15 executions and 9,250 murders. In 1969, there were no executions but murders had increased to 14,590. By 1975, there were no executions but murders continued to rise to 20,510. And in 1980, there were only two executions, compared to the 23,040 murders. The number of annual murders was a 131 percent increase. The murder rate (homicides per 100,000 people) doubled from 5.1 to 10.2. So the murders grew as the number of executions shrank.[10]

From 1995–2000, executions averaged 71 per year, a 21,000 percent increase from the 1965–80 period. The murder rate dropped from 10.2 in 1980 to 5.7 in 1999, a 44 percent reduction.[11]

Response: If capital punishment truly acted as a deterrent, then there should be statistics to support the fact that capital crimes have decreased since the death penalty was introduced. The problem is that statistics can be implemented to show exactly the desired information that was being sought, despite the accuracy of the what the data truly reveals. Many studies reveal an increase in murders with a decrease in executions, but they do not illustrate a causal effect. Furthermore, such studies often include incomplete or inaccurate information, often citing statistics that differ from those of the FBI's Census Bureau regarding murders and executions. Often these studies do not take into account the various states that did or did not have death penalties at the time. Instead, murders are grouped into a national picture, despite what penalties faced criminals in their own state.

There are studies that reveal the exact opposite. In a 1980 study, researcher Thorsten Sellin compared homicide rates over groups of states. Each group of states was similar except in their use of capital punishment. The murder rate should have been lower in death penalty states if capital punishment was a deterrent. However, none of the groups of states showed any deterrence effect.[12] Even Supreme Court Justice Thurgood Marshall said, in a 1989 Amnesty International study, that "the death penalty is no more effective deterrent than life imprisonment."[13]

The simple fact is that there is no irrefutable proof that the threat of capital punishment deters capital crimes. There are too many variables involved. The differences inherent in each court case result in a multitude of different sentences given by judges. The differences in state laws also contribute to an irregularity in the dispensing of justice. Since a simple causal relationship between the existence of capital punishment and occurrence of murders cannot be established, this argument is meaningless.

4. Capital punishment offers few, if any, risks to people who are wrongfully accused.

Argument: Due to the appeals process, those individuals who are wrongfully found guilty of a crime are allowed to have their say in court to produce evidence that will ensure their release. It is one the great things about our judicial system that individuals have the ability to appeal a ruling to a higher court if they feel they have not been justifiably tried and have information to back it up. Besides, with the way the appeals process plays out over a long period of time, it is a relative certainty that an innocent person will have a chance to be exonerated. Couple this with the fact that a very small percentage of people who are sentenced to death ever actually receive the death penalty, and it is obvious that there is almost no risk that an innocent person would ever be put to death.

Response: All it takes is one innocent person put to death to refute this entire argument. One innocent person's life is worth more than having the death penalty in existence. It might be a very unlikely possibility, but it still *is* a possibility.

To put it simply, the death penalty is *irreversible*. Unlike other penalties for crimes, it cannot be undone. According to the American Civil Liberties Union, there has been an average of four cases each year since 1900 in which an innocent person was convicted of murder.[14] Many of these individuals have been sentenced to death. An example is Kirk Bloodsworth, who was sentenced by Maryland in 1985 to death for rape and murder, despite the testimony of a witness. In 1986, his conviction was reversed based on new evidence, but he was re-tried and re-convicted and sentenced to life in prison. In 1993, newly-used DNA evidence proved that Kirk was not the rapist-killer and was released.[15]

A more troubling example is the case of Jesse Tafero, who was convicted in Florida in 1976, along with his wife, Sonia Jacobs, for murdering a state trooper. In 1981, Jacobs' death sentence was reduced on appeal to life imprisonment, and in 1992 her conviction was vacated by a federal court. The evidence on which both Tafero and Jacobs had been convicted and sentenced was identical. However, it had consisted mainly of the perjured testimony of someone seeking a reduced sentence. Tafero was executed in 1990. Due to the arbitrary application of the death penalty and the appeals process, he died while his wife eventually was freed.[16]

5. Capital punishment punishes criminals. It does not discriminate.

Argument: There is no racial or economic discrimination in the application of the death penalty. If it has been shown that a majority of individuals who commit murders are African-American males or those individuals below a certain income, then it is a logical following that more of these individuals are on death row after being convicted of a capital crime.

However, according to 1991 Rand Corporation study by Stephen Klein, white murderers received the death penalty slightly more often (32 percent) than non-white murderers (27 percent).[17] Also, the same study revealed murderers of white victims received the death penalty more often (32 percent) than non-white victims (23 percent). Therefore, there is no racial discrimination.

Response: Again, statistics reveal what an individual wants them to reveal. It makes perfect sense that the *percentages* are roughly equal, but this does not take into account the overall *numbers* of those being sentenced to death and executed. Between 1930 and 1996, 4,220 prisoners were executed in the United States; more than half (53 percent) were African-American.[18]

Statistics from 1995 reveal even more disturbing news regarding the victims of murders.[19] All evidence points to the fact that even in today's society, the killing of white person is treated much more severely than the killing of an African-American person. Between 1977 and 1995, 313 people were executed. Thirty-six were convicted of killing an African-American person while 249 (80 percent) had murdered a white person. Of the 178 white defendants executed, only three had been found guilty of murdering an African-American person.

There is also inequality when it comes to socio-economic class. An adequate defense in capital cases depends on the competency of one's attorneys. Stated plainly, poorer individuals do not have the economic means to hire the best attorneys. Often, they are forced to accept public defenders, who do not have the experience or resources necessary to mount a strong defense.

6. Capital punishment is morally defensible, given its inclusion in the Bible.

Argument: Capital punishment has been around for many years and its inclusion in the Bible supports the fact that it is a morally permissible action. There are the ever present examples of God using capital punishment: Sodom and Gomorrah (Gn 18–19), the first-born sons of the Egyptians (Ex 11), and the Egyptian army in the Red Sea (Ex 14) to name a few. There are also numerous examples in the Old Testament where capital punishment was commanded by God. In Genesis 9:6, God states: "Whoever sheds man's blood, by man his blood shall be shed." Also, Exodus 21:12, Numbers 35:31, and Numbers 35:33 all suggest the permissibility of capital punishment for murder. Moreover, it seems that God allows capital punishment for other crimes as well: rape (Dt 22:25), sodomy (Lv 18:22, 20:13), fornication (Lv 21:9), perjury (Zec 5:4), kidnapping (Ex 21:16), striking or cursing father or mother (Ex 21:15,17, Lv 20:9), disobedience to parents (Dt 21:18–21), theft (Zec 5:3,4), blasphemy (Lv 24:11–14), Sabbath desecration (Ex 35:2), propagating false doctrines (Dt 13:1–10), refusing to abide the decision of the court (Dt 17:12), and homosexuality (Lv 20:13). Surely, God intended there to be capital punishment.

Furthermore, the New Testament teaches about capital punishment. Romans 13:1–7 says that the human government is ordained by God, and that we are to obey government because government does not bear the sword in vain. Human governments are given the responsibility to punish criminals, and this includes murderers who should be sentenced to the death penalty.

Response: Much like statistics, biblical quotation, in the wrong hands, can have a very adverse effect to the intended meaning of the passage. Scripture needs to be viewed in the context of when and why it was written. The Catholic Church's position will be explained in the next section, but for now, let's try to understand the true problem of simply quoting scripture without having a fundamental understanding of the reasons why it was spoken or written in the first place. If we look at various ideas in the Old Testament, a very harsh existence is presented. Many of the topics discussed dealt with specific instances at the time and cannot be applied in the same manner today.

There are numerous examples that illustrate this point. Leviticus 1:9 calls for burning bulls on an altar as a sacrifice. Common sense tells us that such practices are not being called for today. Selling one's offspring into slavery, as mentioned in Exodus 21:7 dealt with a specific issue that was important at the time it was written. It does not mean that parents can offer their son or daughter to the highest bidder. And just because Leviticus 11:10 says it is wrong to eat shellfish does not mean that seafood restaurants are working against the will of God. Certain passages need to be viewed in the context of the issues of the time and location in which they were written.

Church Teaching on Capital Punishment • • • •

- **What is the Catholic Church's position on capital punishment?**

The Catholic Church is, in almost all cases, opposed to capital punishment. The *Catechism of the Catholic Church* states that governments have the right to defend themselves and inflict punishment for crimes but the purpose of that punishment should be to protect society and to correct the guilty party (see *CCC*, 2266).

- **Why is that the position of the Catholic Church?**

The Church believes in the dignity and worth of every human being. Capital punishment allows the government to take the place of God deciding who will live and who will die.

- **What else does the Church teach about capital punishment?**

Pope John Paul II in his encyclical *The Gospel of Life*, states:

> It is clear that, for these purposes [protection of society and rehabilitation of the offender] to be achieved, *the nature and extent of the punishment* must be carefully evaluated and decided upon, and ought not go to the extreme of executing the offender except in cases of absolute necessity: in other words, when it would not be possible otherwise to defend society. Today however, as a result of steady improvements in the organization of the penal system, such cases are very rare, if not practically non-existent (56).

- **Which Scripture passages are relevant to the capital punishment issue?**

Old Testament

As discussed earlier, it is widely thought that the Old Testament supports capital punishment. Supporters of capital punishment frequently cite Exodus 21:23–24 ("But if injury ensues, you shall give life for life, eye for eye, tooth for tooth…."). What is not said is that the Old Testament, in various places, calls for the death penalty for offenses such as being disrespectful toward parents, adultery, and using God's name in vain. The law in Exodus 21 was originally meant to limit punishment to what was best for the community rather than calling for excessive punishment. In the story of Cain and Abel (Genesis 4), when Cain kills his brother, God does not order his death but rather puts a mark on Cain to keep others from harming him.

New Testament

The New Testament is filled with stories of redemption in which sinners came to know the saving love of Jesus and turned their lives around. These scriptural examples should show us that no one is beyond redemption. The parable of the Prodigal Son (Lk 15:11–32) is a shining example. The prodigal son returns to the loving arms of his father after living a life of scandal. Other relevant passages include:

Matthew 5:38

Matthew 7:1–5

Luke 6:35–37

John 8:1–11

Romans 12:14–19

- **What can I do to help stop capital punishment?**
  The means of helping to stop capital punishment are numerous. They include:

  1. Pray.
  2. Get politically involved to help change the laws regarding capital punishment. This could mean writing and meeting your elected representatives at the local, state, and federal levels.
  3. Participate in or start a Pro-life club at your school or in your church.
  4. Discuss the issues with your parents and friends.
  5. Learn about the way capital punishment is carried out in your state or those states around you. Take a trip to the prison on the day of an execution and protest the execution. More importantly, check out information about the existence of prayer vigils in your area or at the prison. If there isn't a prayer vigil, help to start one. Pray for the person being executed, the victims of the crimes, and those who work at the prison who are carrying out the death penalty.

CAPITAL PUNISHMENT DILEMMA #1

George's world has just crashed down around him. His son and daughter were killed when a man broke into their home and shot them in the process of a robbery. The assailant was caught, and a trial was held. The suspect was easily found guilty because of the abundance of evidence left at the scene. Also, a neighbor identified the man as he left the home. There is no question that the man convicted is the killer. Sentencing will begin tomorrow. George is going to be called to the stand for the prosecution. The lawyers want to go for the death penalty, and since the judge is up for election this year, it could pass easily. George is consumed with hate at the sight of the killer. He can't even look at him. Yet tomorrow, the fate of this man will almost assuredly rest with George. The statement he makes will go a long way towards deciding whether this man will live or die. Before this happened, George was strongly against the death penalty.

Discussion Questions:

1) How should George approach his testimony?

2) What responsibility does George have if he testifies and the man is sentenced to die?

3) What is your opinion about the death penalty in this case? in general?

We have discussed this Tough Choice.

_____   _____

Parent/Guardian Signature   Student Signature

CAPITAL PUNISHMENT DILEMMA #2

Jimmy was a single father of a mildly retarded girl, Gabby. He cared for her every need, helped her cope with the outside world, and supported her. Pretty soon, she became his sole reason for living. As she became a teenager, he allowed her more and more freedom. One day, he let her go to the mall pet store on her own while he went to buy the two of them sodas. In those brief seven or eight minutes, she was abducted from the store. The next day her body was found along a roadside. A convicted child molester was charged with the crime. At the pretrial hearing the man smirked at Jimmy. Jimmy was filled with rage. The next day Jimmy returned to the courthouse with a razor-sharp plastic knife. During a lull in the proceedings, he lunged at the man and stabbed him in the neck. The man died instantly. Jimmy was now charged with murder. Anita is the jury foreman. She is a prominent leader in the area and is respected by the other members of the jury. She has great influence over the other jurors on the case.

Discussion Questions:

1) From the information given, should Jimmy be convicted of murder?

2) Would you have favored the death penalty for the man who killed Jimmy's daughter? What about for Jimmy?

3) Is it ever excusable to strike out against another in anger? Explain.

We have discussed this Tough Choice.

_____

Parent/Guardian Signature

_____

Student Signature

Notes

1. "Capital Punishment," *The Columbia Electronic Encyclopedia,* http://www.infoplease.com/ce6/society/A0857171.html

2. http://sun.soci.niu.edu/~critcrim/dp/states.using.txt from PEACENET's Prison Information Desk: http://www.peacenet.apc.org/prisons/issues/dp.html

3. Capital Punishment FAQs from ASC's Critical Criminology Division, http://sun.soci.niu.edu/~critcrim/dp/faq/rapeexec.html

4. http://www.law.onu.edu/faculty/streib/juvdeath.htm

5. http://sun.soci.niu.edu/~critcrim/dp/faq/retard.txt, from Death Penalty Information Center

6. U.S. Government Accounting Office, *Limited Data Available in Costs of Death Sentences* (1989): 50.

7. http://www.personal.umich.edu/~spragge/capital.html

8. Ibid.

9. http://www.wesleylowe.com/cp.html

10. Ibid.

11. Ibid. Quotation from Dudley Sharp, of the criminal-justice reform group, Justice For All

12. Thorsten Sellin. *The Penalty of Death,* (Beverly Hills: Sage, 1980): 139–156.

13. Amnesty International. *When the State Kills…The Death Penalty v. Human Rights* (London: Amnesty, 1989): 13.

14. Radelet, Lofquist, and Bedau, in *Thomas M. Cooley Law Review* (1997); Radelet, Bedau, and Putnam, *In Spite of Innocence* (1992); Bedau and Radelet, "Miscarriage of Justice in Potentially Capital Cases," in *Stanford Law Review* (1987).

15. http://archive.aclu.org/library/case_against_death.html

16. Ibid, and Radelet, Lofquist, and Bedau, in *Thomas M. Cooley Law Review* (1997).

17. http://www.wesleylowe.com/cp.html

18. Bureau of Justice Statistics, "Capital Punishment 1977" and "Death Row USA," Summer 1996.

19. "Death Row USA," Summer 1996 and *Sourcebook of Criminal Justice Statistics—1995.*

CHILD ABUSE &
DOMESTIC VIOLENCE
CHILD ABUSE &
DOMESTIC VIOLENCE
CHILD ABUSE &
DOMESTIC VIOLENCE
CHILD ABUSE &
DOMESTIC VIOLENCE

CHILD ABUSE &
DOMESTIC VIOLENCE

CHILD ABUSE &
DOMESTIC VIOLENCE
CHILD ABUSE &
DOMESTIC VIOLENCE
CHILD ABUSE &
DOMESTIC VIOLENCE
CHILD ABUSE &
DOMESTIC VIOLENCE
CHILD ABUSE &
DOMESTIC VIOLENCE
CHILD ABUSE &
DOMESTIC VIOLENCE
CHILD ABUSE &
DOMESTIC VIOLENCE
CHILD ABUSE &
DOMESTIC VIOLENCE

Overview of the Child Abuse and Domestic Violence Issues • • • • • • • • • • • • • • • •

- **What is child abuse?**

  Child abuse is the nonaccidental injury or pattern of injuries to a child.[1] Child abuse includes the following: nonaccidental physical injury, neglect, sexual molestation, and emotional abuse.

- **What is domestic violence?**

  Domestic violence is a pattern of assaulting and coercing behaviors, including physical, sexual, and psychological attacks, as well as economic coercion, that adults or adolescents use against their intimate partners.[2] Domestic violence mainly involves violence directed by a husband against his wife, or a live-in boyfriend against his girlfriend.

- **How common are these problems?**

  Child Abuse

  In a recent year, nearly four million children were reported for child abuse and neglect to various child protective service (CPS) agencies across the nation. Between 1988 and 1997, child abuse reporting levels have increased 41 percent. Roughly 47 out of every 1,000 children are reported as victims of child abuse.[3] In 1998, an estimated 1,100 children died of abuse and neglect—an average of more than three children per day. Of these children, more than 75 percent were under the age of five and 38 percent were under the age of one.[4]

  Domestic Violence

  Reports on exact numbers regarding domestic violence differ, due to the lack of reporting of this crime. However, the following statistics illustrate how large a problem this is:

  > A 1995 survey found that 31 percent of women said that they were victims of domestic abuse.[5] Estimates of women abused by a spouse or live-in partner range from 960,000 incidents[6] to 3,900,000 per year.[7]
  >
  > According to the FBI Uniform Crime Statistics from 1996, 1,500 women in this country are murdered by husbands or boyfriends each year.

- **What are the long-term effects of child abuse and domestic violence on children?**

  Children from violent homes have an increased risk of drug and alcohol abuse and juvenile delinquency. They may experience learning, language, and developmental problems.[8] In addition, they may develop the following characteristics: low self-esteem, aggressiveness, anxiety, poor health, distrust of relationships, guilt, desensitization to pain, self-abuse, depression, anger, avoidance, mood swings, and anti-social behavior.

  Boys who witness domestic violence are four times more likely to become batterers of female partners as adults, twenty-five times more likely to commit rape as an adult, six times more likely to commit suicide, 74 percent more likely to commit crimes, and 24 times more likely to commit sexual assault.[9]

  Girls from homes in which domestic violence occurs are 6.5 times more likely to be sexually assaulted and are more likely to become pregnant as a teen.[10]

- **What are the signs of child abuse?[11]**
  Signs of child abuse can be divided into three categories:

  1. *Physical signs*—crying or attempting to avoid going with the abuser or to a place where abuse occurred, bruises, cuts, burns, broken bones, or repeated injuries.
  2. *Emotional signs*—shunning affection, overly clingy, extreme behaviors, acting inappropriately (infantile or adult-like), reducing or stopping communication, unexplained illnesses.
  3. *Sexual signs*—difficulty walking or sitting, reluctance to remove outer clothing (sweaters/coats), wearing extra clothing, exhibiting sexual curiosity not normally associated with their developmental age.

- **What help is available for suspected cases of domestic violence and child abuse?**
  In an emergency, call 9-1-1. Other resources include:

  National Domestic Violence/Abuse Hotline
  1-800-799-7233
  (1-800-799-SAFE)

  Childhelp USA's National Child Abuse Hotline
  1-800-422-4453
  (1-800-4ACHILD)

Church Teaching on Child Abuse and Domestic Violence

- **What does the Church teach about domestic violence and child abuse?**

  While the Church does not use the terms "domestic violence" and "child abuse," it unquestionably teaches that all people are to be respected and to live free of the fear of violence against them. This is especially true within the context of the family. Several relevant paragraphs in the *Catechism of the Catholic Church* apply, including:

  CCC 2203

  CCC 2222

  CCC 2223

- **Why is that the teaching of the Catholic Church?**

  All people are to be treated with dignity and respect. Both domestic violence and child abuse are examples of people exhibiting violent or psychological power over another in an unjust manner. On the subject of child abuse, it does not mean that parents cannot discipline their children but that discipline has limits.

- **Which Scripture passages are relevant to the child abuse and domestic violence issue?**

  Sirach 30: 1–2

  Ephesians 6:4

CHILD ABUSE &
DOMESTIC VIOLENCE DILEMMA #1

Steve and Mark have been friends for years. Growing up, each had spent a great deal of time in the other's house. Lately, Mark has been noticing that they have spent an increasing amount of time at his house, instead of Steve's. One day, when picking up Steve for school, Mark noticed bruises down Steve's mom's arm and across the side of her face. As soon as Steve got into the car, Mark asked him what had happened to his mom. Steve tried to change the subject, but Mark's persistence got him to reveal what was really going on: Steve's father was abusive to Steve's mother. He told Mark that if the truth got out, the beatings would only get worse. Besides, Steve said this was something he and his mom had learned to live with.

Discussion Questions:

1) What should Mark do?

2) Would your response be different if it was a child that was being beaten? How?

3) Does a friend's request not to tell weigh into the decision? Why or why not?

4) What are the short-term and long-term problems if this is allowed to continue?

5) Are families allowed privacy around an issue like this? Why or why not?

We have discussed this Tough Choice.

_____

Parent/Guardian Signature

_____

Student Signature

CHILD ABUSE &
DOMESTIC VIOLENCE DILEMMA #2

Mitch is in Will's first period chemistry class. Will knows that Mitch and his dad do not get along well, and he has been in their house during a few of the confrontations. The yelling and distress caused by the situation has often caused Will to leave early. In recent weeks they have been fighting more because of Mitch's poor grades. Will heard Mitch's dad tell him that he had one more chance to improve his grade in chemistry, "or else". Mitch got a "D" on his third quarter report card. On the day after report cards were sent home Mitch came to school with a red mark under his eye. Will asked him what happened. Mitch said that he did not want to talk about it and ignored Will for the rest of the period.

Discussion Questions:

1) What should Will do?

2) How would you define child abuse in your own words?

3) Who should Will talk to?

4) Does Will have the right to pry into Mitch's family situation?

5) Suppose Mitch's father has been prosecuted for abuse before. Does knowing that Mitch will be placed in a foster home change the situation?

We have discussed this Tough Choice.

_____

Parent/Guardian Signature

_____

Student Signature

Notes

1. http://www.childabuse.com/fs20.htm

2. Ibid.

3. C.T. Wang and Daro D. Wang. *Current Trends in Child Abuse Reporting and Fatalities: The Results of the 1997 Annual Fifty State Survey* (Chicago, IL: Prevent Child Abuse America, 1998).

4. U.S. Department of Health and Human Services, Children's Bureau, *Child Maltreatment 1998: Reports from the States to the National Child Abuse and Neglect Data System (NCANDS* (Washington, D.C.: U.S. Government Printing Office, 2000). Online statistical fact sheets: www.calib.com/nccanch/stats/index.cfm

5. Lieberman Research Inc. *Domestic violence advertising campaign tracking survey*, Wave 3, November 1995. (San Francisco, CA: Family Violence Prevention Fund and The Advertising Council, 1996).

6. U.S. Department of Justice, "Violence by Intimates: Analysis of Data on Crimes by Current or Former Spouses, Boyfriends, and Girlfriends" (March 1998).

7. The Commonwealth Fund, "First Comprehensive National Health Survey of American Women," July 1993.

8. *Domestic Violence—A Guide for Health Care Professionals*, State of New Jersey, Department of Community Affairs, March 1990.

9. A Safe Place: Lake County Crisis Center, P.O. Box 1067, Waukegan, IL 60079 at http://www.asafeplaceforhelp.org/childwitnesses2.html

10. Ibid.

11. http://injuryboard.com/specificArticleFromSiteSearch.cfm?Article=271

DIVORCE
DIVORCE
DIVORCE
DIVORCE
DIVORCE
DIVORCE

DIVORCE

DIVORCE
DIVORCE
DIVORCE
DIVORCE
DIVORCE
DIVORCE
DIVORCE
DIVORCE
DIVORCE
DIVORCE
DIVORCE
DIVORCE
DIVORCE
DIVORCE
DIVORCE

Overview of Divorce Issues • • • • • • • • • • •

- **What is divorce?**
Divorce is defined as the legal and formal dissolution of marriage by the state.

- **About how many divorces are there annually in the United States?**
In a recent year, there were 1,163,000 divorces in the United States.[1] In this same year, there was a 43 percent chance that all new marriages would end in divorce.[2]

- **How long do most marriages last?**
Using the same statistics, the average length of a marriage was 7.2 years.[3]

- **How many children of divorced couples are there?**
Each year, there are roughly one million children from new divorces.[4] Roughly 24 percent of married households have children, while 27 percent of households with children have only one parent.[5] Twenty million children under the age of eighteen are living with just one parent.[6]

- **Don't the divorce statistics indicate that people should live together first to see if they are compatible with one another?**
No, in fact, quite the opposite is true. Living together before marriage, or cohabitation, actually leads to more instances of divorce than for couples choosing to live separately until marriage. There are roughly 3.8 million cohabiting couples.[7] For these couples, the risk of divorce is almost double that of those who did not live together.[8]

- **What are some of the reasons people get divorced?**
There are numerous reasons for each situation in which a couple decides to get divorced, and therefore it would be impossible to list all of them. However, in 1999, the Australian Institute of Family Studies conducted a study that offered four areas of conclusions: affective issues, abusive behaviors, external pressures, and other factors.[9]

By far, the biggest reasons people gave for divorce were affective reasons. These affective reasons were communication problems (27.3 percent), incompatibility or "drifting apart" (21 percent), and infidelity (20 percent). Abusive behaviors were the next most common response given with physical violence to spouse or child (5.5 percent), alcohol/drug abuse (7.4 percent), and emotional and/or verbal abuse (1.9 percent) representing this demographic. External pressures, such as financial problems (4.7 percent), work/time (2.7 percent), family interference (0.6 percent), and physical/mental health (4.7 percent), came next. Finally, other factors like spouse's personality (1.1 percent), children's problems (1.4 percent), and various other random cases (1.4 percent), rounded out the list.

What do these statistics tell us? Well, if one were to weed through all these numbers, one could see that there are a few simple reasons why so many divorces occur. It is our contention that so many divorces occur due to three important factors and the inter-connection between these three factors: age of the spouse(s), mutual knowledge of the spouse(s), and commitment to the institution/sacrament of marriage.

Age plays a role in divorce because many times, couples choose to get married at a very young age. While this is not necessarily a bad thing, sometimes this takes place before the two people have had a chance to develop as individuals. Hopefully, they will develop together, along the same direction and life path, but oftentimes, their development changes who they are and the two individuals mature in a way that leads them apart. Statistics back this point up: 40 percent of people who married under the age of twenty eventually get divorced compared to 24 percent who married over the age of twenty-five.[10] Couples must be mature, developed, and content with who they are as individuals before they are able to give themselves to one another in marriage.

Second, and tied to the age problem, is the knowledge of the spouse. Due to technological innovation, career opportunities, and a decentralized ethnic family base, the world has become smaller. People are free to move and seek out their calling far from where they were born. This means that people no longer live in areas surrounded by those with whom they have grown up. Therefore, it is less likely that an individual will marry someone they knew while growing up, and it is that much more difficult to know an individual prior to marriage, unless a substantial amount of time has been spent with that person. Short-term dating and engagement periods are becoming all to common, which results in the unfortunate byproduct of people not truly knowing their spouses before getting married. While the amount of time required to truly *know* an individual is different in every case, it should be given top priority before something as serious and as sacred as marriage is considered.

Combined with these first two factors is the third, a commitment to the institution/sacrament of marriage. In previous generations, it was common for a man and a woman to be married for life. Today, it is not so. What is of equal concern is that sometimes even the *expectation* of marriage is not for life. This results from people's views on the institution/sacrament of marriage. As we have mentioned, nearly a million children each year become acquainted with divorce. As the idea of living in a divorced household becomes more commonplace in these children's minds, the expectation that this is not out-of the ordinary, but rather a fact of life develops.

This idea may fester throughout their lives, so when the time comes for them to get married, the idea that divorce is a legitimate alternative is already firmly planted in their mentality. Couple this with what takes place in our society today. Much of what is done is constructed to serve the individual's needs in a quick manner. Fast food, remote controls, the Internet, and other beneficial features in our society also possess an inherent quality of creating in individuals the mindset that personal satisfaction is to be obtained without much effort and in a very short time period. This attitude flies in the face of any committed relationship. Every relationship, especially marriage, involves struggles, fears, discoveries, growth apart, reconciliation, development as individuals, and development together. Marriage is a process, not an endgame. Just because a couple decides to get married does not mean that life will no longer pose any challenges. It simply means that an individual is open to exploring those challenges with another person. If marriage is seen in this light, then any obstacles that present themselves to a married couple do not become reasons for a quick and easy separation but rather reasons to pursue any and all means to work together to grow in love and deepen the marriage commitment. Therefore marriage needs to be seen as lifelong and any inherent struggles are not reasons to give up, but to push forward.

If we look at these three factors, we can see how they figure into the reasoning given by most people for divorce. Communication, incompatibility, infidelity, abuse, financial and work reasons, family interference, spousal personality, and many others all can be tied to age, knowledge of the spouse, and commitment to the institution/sacrament of marriage. Knowing yourself and your interests comes first. It allows you to be fully conscious of what you offer to another. Learning about and understanding your spouse comes next. Taking the time to find out the joys, sorrows, motivations, and struggles of your partner in a variety of situations and emotional states will prepare two people for what to expect in marriage. Finally, truly believing and taking to heart the words "for richer or poorer, in good times and in bad, in sickness and in health," is the final piece of the puzzle. If couples share a common mindset on and commitment to marriage, they will be open to whatever life has to offer. By keeping these three factors in mind, there is hope for decreasing the occurrence of divorce while upholding the sanctity of marriage.

Church Teaching on Divorce • • • • • • • • • • • •

- **What is the Catholic Church's position on divorce?**

The Catholic Church holds that God intended marriages to be "indissoluble" or permanent. It holds marriage as a sacrament and thus promises are made before God and the Church. The *Catechism of the Catholic Church* states: "A ratified and consummated marriage cannot be dissolved by any human power for any reason other than death" (2382). The Church does teach that separation of spouses while still maintaining the marriage bond is acceptable in certain cases. Thus "civil divorce" is acceptable if issues such as legal rights, care of the children, or the protection of inheritance is at stake.

- **Why is that the position of the Catholic Church?**

The Church calls divorce a "grave offense" because "it claims to break the contract, to which the spouses freely consented, to live with each other until death." Remarrying, even when recognized by civil law, adds to the gravity of the offense because the remarried person is in a situation of both "public and permanent adultery" because in the eyes of God, he or she is still married to another.

- **What is an annulment?**

An annulment is a declaration by the Church that a marriage is invalid. It is an official judgment that a sacramental marriage never took place, in spite of all appearances. For example, an annulment can be granted if the Church deems that one or both members of the couple did not freely enter into the marriage.

- **Which Scripture passages are relevant to the issue of divorce?**

Matthew 5: 31–32

Matthew 19:3–9

Mark 10: 9–12

Luke 16:18

I Corinthians 7:10–11

DIVORCE DILEMMA #1

Lisa's family has always been a close-knit group. Her parents have been very active at the school, in their parish, and in the community. They host parties for nearly every holiday or special occasion, and they are well respected by the parents of their children's classmates. Rachel has been one of Lisa's close friends during their high school years. They have seen each other through many highs and lows. Lately, Lisa has been a little down because of what she calls "family problems". Rachel is a surprised at this admission, considering that most people feel Lisa's family is the model family.

Last week, Lisa told Rachel that her parents are getting divorced. For the past week, Rachel has had to console Lisa inside and outside of school because Lisa has been very emotional. Much of the time involves Rachel answering Lisa's questions, like: "Why is this happening?" "Is this something I did?" "How could I have prevented this?" and "How am I going to grow up without two parents in the house?" Rachel wants to be supportive, but her lack of experience with divorce means she has little knowledge of what Lisa can expect.

Discussion Questions:

1) What could Rachel do or say?

2) Why do people get divorced?

3) Do you know of people whose parents are divorced? Discuss their experience.

4) Is there such a thing as an "ideal" or "perfect" marriage?

5) What is your opinion of marriage? What should an ideal marriage involve?

6) To whom can children turn when faced with the prospect of divorce?

We have discussed this Tough Choice.

_____   _____

Parent/Guardian Signature   Student Signature

DIVORCE DILEMMA #2

Tonya and Mark are good friends. Mark respects Tonya a great deal and often asks for Tonya's opinion on various matters. Also, they have been there for each other during tough times. Mark supported Tonya when her brother died. Tonya provided a shoulder to lean on and ear to listen when Mark's parents were going through their divorce. Mark now lives with his mother, but he is able to see his father every other weekend.

Lately, Mark has been complaining about his mother. Tonya knows that Mark's mother is a good person who looks out for Mark's best interests. She has certain expectations of Mark and enforces her policies. Mark's father is the exact opposite. He allows Mark to do whatever he wants. He also buys expensive gifts for Mark, even when Mark's mother specifically asks him to refrain from doing so. Mark has confided in Tonya that he would much rather live with his father because his mother is so mean to him. There is a court appointment coming up next week in which Mark wants to ask the judge to give custody to his father instead of his mother. Tonya knows that Mark's opinion is biased, but she also knows that he has a great love for his father, and she would not want to alter that perception for Mark.

Discussion Questions:

1) What should Tonya do?

2) What does it mean to be a good parent?

3) How much should parents try to be "friends" with their children?

4) What happens when one parent acts in opposition to the wishes of the other parent?

5) How can children of divorced parents show their loyalty and love to each parent without offending the other?

We have discussed these Tough Choices.

_____

Parent/Guardian Signature

_____

Student Signature

Notes

1. Statistics compiled by the U.S. Census Bureau, National Center for Health Statistics, Americans for Divorce Reform, Centers for Disease Control and Prevention, Institute for Equality in Marriage, American Association for Single People, Ameristat, Public Agenda, found at http://www.divorcemagazine.com/statistics/statsUS.shtml

2. Ibid.

3. Ibid.

4. Ibid.

5. Ibid.

6. Ibid.

7. Ibid.

8. Bumpass & Sweet 1995; Hall & Zhao 1995; Bracher, Santow, Morgan & Russell 1993; DeMaris & Rao 1992 and Glenn 1990, found at http://members.aol.com/cohabitating/facts.htm

9. Ilene Wolcott and Jody Hughes, "Towards Understanding the Reasons for Divorce," Australian Institute of Family Studies (AIFS) 1999. Found at http://www.aifs.org.au/institute/pubs/WP20.html

10. http://www.divorcemagazine.com/statistics/statsUS.shtml

DRUGS & ALCOHOL
DRUGS & ALCOHOL
DRUGS & ALCOHOL
DRUGS & ALCOHOL
DRUGS & ALCOHOL
DRUGS & ALCOHOL

DRUGS & ALCOHOL

DRUGS & ALCOHOL
DRUGS & ALCOHOL
DRUGS & ALCOHOL
DRUGS & ALCOHOL
DRUGS & ALCOHOL
DRUGS & ALCOHOL
DRUGS & ALCOHOL
DRUGS & ALCOHOL
DRUGS & ALCOHOL
DRUGS & ALCOHOL
DRUGS & ALCOHOL
DRUGS & ALCOHOL
DRUGS & ALCOHOL
DRUGS & ALCOHOL
DRUGS & ALCOHOL
DRUGS & ALCOHOL
DRUGS & ALCOHOL

Overview of Drugs and Alcohol Issues   • • • • •

- **Is alcohol a drug?**

    Yes, alcohol is a drug, due to its chemical make-up and the definition of drugs. A drug, by definition, is any substance that kills or inactivates germs, affects any body function or organ, or acts as a narcotic or hallucinogen, especially one that is habit forming.

- **How does alcohol affect the body?**

    All alcoholic beverages contain ethanol, or ethyl alcohol, which is often referred to as alcohol. Alcohol is a sedative hypnotic that acts as a depressant to the central nervous system. When someone drinks alcohol, it flows into the stomach. Twenty percent of the alcohol is absorbed through the stomach while the remaining 80 percent is absorbed through the small intestine and carried by the bloodstream to the other vital organs of the body, where it is absorbed.[1] The higher the concentration of the alcoholic content in the drink, the quicker it is absorbed.

    Alcohol "depresses", or slows down, the functioning of the body's cells and organs until they are less efficient. It influences the brain by affecting the coordination of senses, perception, speech, and judgment. As it depresses body functions, it can lessen inhibitions. For this reason, people sometimes erroneously believe alcohol is a stimulant. It is not. What actually happens is that emotions are more easily expressed when the part of the brain responsible for behavior is depressed or relaxed, leading to an exhilaration of emotions. If enough alcohol is consumed, the drinker can fall asleep or lapse into a coma.

- **How is the amount of alcohol in the body measured?**

    The drinker's blood alcohol level (BAL) or blood alcohol content/concentration (BAC) rises the more alcohol is consumed. It is based on the relationship between the amount of blood parts containing alcohol when compared to the overall number of blood parts.[2] For example, a 0.07 BAC indicates about seven parts alcohol per 10,000 parts other blood components. By consuming more alcohol than the body can eliminate, alcohol accumulates in the bloodstream and the BAC rises.

- **Do factors besides alcohol affect the blood alcohol concentration (BAC) and emotional and physical state of a person?**

    Yes, a person's BAC and effects of alcohol on an individual can be affected by: how one feels before drinking, what the drinker expects alcohol to do, age, gender, body weight, general health, and fitness, the amount of time it takes to consume a drink, food in the stomach, and experience with alcoholic beverages.[3] If one's emotional state is extreme (upset, tired, excited, sad, nervous, happy), the person may gulp drinks and consume more alcohol than intended. If it is a drinker's anticipation that alcohol will make them feel a certain way, alcohol will enhance those feelings. Older people will have higher BACs for the same amount of drinks due to the fact that the capacity of the liver to process alcohol decreases with age.[4] Women have less water and more fat in their bodies compared to men, so when they drink alcohol, their BAC rises more quickly.[5]

    Because a person with a smaller body size has less water in their body than someone with a larger body size, BAC will rise more quickly in smaller people. Health conditions affecting the liver or stomach can slow the rate the BAC decreases. Spacing out drinks over time will allow alcohol to be processed through the body and eliminated, creating a lower BAC than in individuals who drink the same amount of drinks in a shorter time frame. The BAC of someone who drinks on an empty stomach increases faster than someone who has eaten a large meal due to the fact that a full stomach slows the absorption of alcohol in the small intestine. Finally, prior experience with alcohol not only prepares a person for what to expect, but may also cause them to feel less effects from alcohol for the same quantity consumed.

- **What is the relationship of number of drinks to bodily impairment?**

Again, this depends on many of the factors listed above. Alcohol affects individuals differently and even varies in its effects on the same individual at different times. If averages are assumed, certain estimates can be made per hour. For purposes of quantifying alcoholic intake, one drink equals one can or bottle of beer, one glass of wine or wine cooler, one shot of liquor, or one mixed drink containing liquor.

The Center of Alcohol Studies[6] reports that in a person weighing 150 lbs.:

> A BAC of 0.03 percent (one drink) causes the drinker to feel relaxed and experience a slight feeling of exhilaration.
> A BAC of 0.06 percent (two drinks) causes the drinker to feel warm and relaxed and includes a decrease of fine motor skills. The person is less concerned with minor irritations.
> A BAC of 0.09 percent (three drinks) slows a person's reaction time, inhibits muscle control, slurs speech, and causes their legs to feel wobbly.
> A BAC of 0.12 percent (four drinks) alters a drinker's judgment, lessens their inhibitions and self-restraint, and impairs reasoning and logical decision-making ability.
> A BAC of 0.15 percent (five drinks) blurs an individual's vision, hampers their speech, causes unsteady gait, and impairs coordination.
> A BAC of 0.18 percent (six drinks) impairs the drinker's behavior and makes it difficult for him or her to stay awake.
> A BAC of 0.30 percent (10–12 drinks) puts the drinker into a deep sleep or coma.
> A BAC of 0.50 percent puts a person into a deep coma.
> A BAC of 1.0 percent paralyzes the breathing center in the brain and causes death.

- **What is binge drinking? How common is it among teenagers?**

A "binge drinker" as defined by the National Clearinghouse for Alcohol and Drug Information is someone who has five or more drinks on the same occasion on at least one day in the past thirty days. In 2000, almost seven million people between ages 12 and 20 admitted to binge drinking, which translates to one in every five people (20 percent) under the legal drinking age.[7]

- **What are some of the consequences of underage alcohol use?**

Alcohol is the most widely used drug among teenagers. Its use is associated with risk-taking and sensation-seeking behavior. There are negative consequences associated with alcohol ingestion, namely: physical and mental health problems, decreased academic performance, commission of crime, or death.[8] Other statistics related to this issue include:

Physical and Mental Health Problems
Individuals who drink before they are fifteen years old are four times as likely to develop alcohol dependence as those who defer drinking until the age of twenty-one. For each additional year that drinking is delayed, the probability of developing an alcohol dependence decreases by fourteen percent.[9]
Much like adults, teenagers who drink heavily risk developing cirrhosis of the liver, hemorrhagic stroke, and certain types of cancer.[10]
Adolescents using alcohol are more likely to be sexually active at an earlier age, to have sex more often, and to engage in unprotected sex, increasing their risk of HIV and other sexually transmitted diseases.[11]
Youngsters that abuse alcohol are four times more likely to experience major depression.[12]

Decreased Academic Performance

Even small doses of alcohol damage a young brain more rapidly than they damage a mature brain. Exposure to alcohol during adolescence reduces the ability to learn.[13]

Alcohol problems are cited in more than 40 percent of all college cases involving academic problems and are the reasons given by 28 percent of all college dropouts.[14]

High school students who use alcohol or other substances are five times more likely to drop out of high school than other students.[15]

Commission of Crime

Of all violent crime on college campuses, 95 percent is alcohol related. 90 percent of all college rapes involve alcohol use by the victim and/or the assailant.[16]

Death

In 1997, 21 percent of 15–20 year old drivers killed in accidents were under the influence of alcohol.[17]

Drowning is the leading cause of death for adolescents and young adults. Nearly 50 percent of young males who drown had been drinking. An equal percentage killed during diving accidents are alcohol-related.[18]

Roughly 240,000–360,000 (2 to 3 percent) of the 12,000,000 college undergraduates in our country die from alcohol-related causes.[19]

- **Why is nicotine a drug? How does it affect the body?**

Cigarette smoke contains thousands of substances. The addictive drug in cigarette smoke is nicotine. Nicotine is a natural part of the tobacco leaf. In larger amounts, nicotine is a deadly poison. One drop of purified nicotine on the tongue will kill a person. Nicotine affects the brain and central nervous system. The smoker inhales and draws nicotine into the lungs. In less than seven seconds, it is picked up by the bloodstream and pumped by the heart to the brain. The sudden burst of nicotine produces an instant "high". It also affects other areas of the body. Nicotine makes the heart beat faster, which, in turn, increases a person's rate of breathing and causes that individual to use more oxygen. It also causes blood vessels to narrow, and blood flows through them more slowly. This effect can increase blood pressure and increase the likelihood of the blood clotting.

- **What are the long-term effects of nicotine use?**

Some of the long-term effects of nicotine use are:

Chronic bronchitis—Smoking causes inflammation of the cells lining the inside of the bronchi, air passages connecting the windpipe (trachea) with the sacs of the lung (alveoli), where oxygen is taken up by the blood. This inflammation causes excessive production of mucus and swelling of the bronchial walls, obstructing airflow in and out of the lungs. The cilia lining the air passages become paralyzed by the mucus. Germs, which are normally removed by the cilia, accumulate and cause an inflammation of the walls of the air passages.

Emphysema—Prolonged smoking irritates the bronchi, which destroys the normal elasticity of the air sacs and walls of the airways. People with emphysema must forcibly blow air out in order to empty the lungs. However, forcing air out puts pressure on the airways, compressing them and causing them to collapse, even tearing the walls of air sacs. Collapsing and tearing of the walls causes the lungs to become enlarged and less efficient at moving air in and contaminants out of the lungs. The destruction of the air sac walls means less surface area for gas exchange. This means a person will have difficulty breathing and that the heart must work harder to circulate blood through the lungs. This means oxygen is less available to the body.

Lung Cancer—The carcinogenic substances found in cigarettes cause a mutation of the cells lining the air passages. This mutation causes the cells to divide uncontrollably, leading to cancerous growth.

Heart Disease—The inhalation of carbon monoxide causes the hemoglobin in the blood to bond with carbon monoxide instead of oxygen. When the body lacks oxygen, the heart must work harder. When combined with narrowing blood vessels and decreased oxygen intake, the constant strain on the heart leads to cardiac disease and ultimately heart failure.

Stroke—As previously described, smoking causes the blood vessels to narrow and stiffen. This compromises the function of all body organs. In the brain, narrowed arteries and sluggish circulation increase the opportunity of the blood to clot and occlude multiple vessels. The decreased supply of oxygenated blood to either the heart or brain causes cellular death, which leads to heart attack or stroke.

- **How common is cigarette smoking among teenagers?**

According to American Lung Association statistics from June of 2002, an estimated 4.5 million adolescents are cigarette smokers.[20] Close to 4,800 teenagers (ages 11 to 17) begin smoking every day, and of these, nearly 2,000 will become habitual smokers.[21] This translates to roughly two million new teenage smokers each year. Twenty-eight percent of all high-school students in the country use cigarettes.[22] Nine out of ten overall smokers indicated that they began smoking before they turned 21 years old.[23]

Another interesting phenomenon is how many teenage smokers did not expect to become addicted to cigarettes and how many wish they had never started. Only 5 percent of regular smokers surveyed in high school believed that they would be smoking five years later. Between seven and nine years later, nearly 75 percent were still smoking.[24] Also, 70 percent of smokers age 12 to 17 regret their decision to start smoking, and 66 percent admit that they want to quit.[25]

- **Why is marijuana a drug? How does it affect the body?**

Marijuana is a mixture of leaves, stems, and seeds from the *cannabis sativa* plant. The main mind-altering chemical found in marijuana is delta-9-tetrahydrocannabinol, or THC. However, there are more than 400 other chemicals in marijuana, including many of the same cancer causing chemicals found in cigarette smoke, such as: carbon monoxide, carbon dioxide, acetone, benzene, toluene, vinyl chloride, dimethylnitrosamine, methylethylnitrosamine, benz(a)anthracene, benz(a)pyrene, ammonia, and hydrogen cyanide.[26] Much like alcohol and nicotine, marijuana is an addictive drug that causes users to build up a tolerance.[27]

Once inhaled, marijuana smoke quickly travels to the other organs of the body via the bloodstream. Its chemical similarity to cigarettes explains the effects it has on the lungs. In the brain, THC gathers on the receptor nerve cells and alters the way these cells function. It affects the hippocampus, which controls short-term memory, and the cerebral cortex, which controls thinking and concentrating.[28] Therefore, THC makes it hard for the user to recall recent events, to perform tasks requiring short-term memory, or to participate in activities that involve more than one step. Marijuana also causes the heart to beat faster, alters a person's sense of time, and hampers coordination.

In addition to the same long-term effects as smoking, prolonged marijuana use causes other disorders. Marijuana causes a multitude of psychological disorders, including acute toxic psychosis, panic attacks, flashbacks, delusions, depersonalization, hallucinations, paranoia, depression, and aggression.[29] It can lead to the development of amotivational syndrome, causing the person to be apathetic, lose the ability to set realistic goals, and decrease drive and ambition[30]. Marijuana users are six times more likely to develop schizophrenia than non-users.[31] In males, smoking marijuana lowers testosterone production and sperm count, and in females, it disrupts hormone cycles.[32] If used by pregnant mothers, it can cause low birth weight in babies.[33] Marijuana makes the user more likely to advance to more potent drugs. Approximately 20 percent of people who use marijuana between 3 and 10 times go on to use cocaine. About 75 percent of people that use marijuana 100 times or more will use cocaine.[34]

- **How is marijuana used? What are the slang terms for marijuana?**

Most marijuana users will roll loose marijuana into a cigarette, called a joint or a nail, or smoke it in a pipe. Some choose to use a water pipe, known as a bong. Others cut open a cigar and replace the tobacco inside the cigar with marijuana, creating what's known as a blunt. Smoking a blunt coupled with drinking a 40 oz. bottle of malt liquor is known as a B-40. Marijuana can also be mixed with food or brewed into a tea.

Much like anything else, marijuana has many slang terms that change with time and with respect to location. There are standard terms such as pot, weed, Mary Jane, grass, reefer, herb, and ganja. Additional terms such as chronic, endo, skunk, boom, Aunt Mary, gangster, kif, Texas Tea, and Maui wowie are also used.[35]

- **How common is marijuana use among teenagers?**

Comparisons from recent years by the University of Michigan's Institute for Social Research reveal that marijuana use is common among high-school students. The number of high-school seniors who have tried marijuana was 41.7 percent in 1995, 44.9 percent in 1996, 49.6 percent in 1997, and has relatively stayed the same during the past few years.

Church Teaching on Drugs and Alcohol • • • •

- **What is the Catholic Church's position on drugs and alcohol?**

  The Church teaches that morality requires "respect for the life of the body" (*CCC*, 2289). The Church calls us each "to avoid every kind of excess" which includes the abuse of food, alcohol, tobacco, or medicine. Excessive use of alcohol is related to gluttony, one of the seven deadly sins.

  On the issue of drugs the Church teaches that drugs cause great harm to individuals and society as a whole. According to the *Catechism:* "Their [drugs] use, except on strictly therapeutic grounds, is a grave offense" (2291).

- **Why is that the position of the Catholic Church?**

  The Church calls each person to treat his or her body as a temple of the Holy Spirit (see 1 Cor 6:19). Using substances that contribute to the decline of our health and the well being of others must be avoided. The abuse of drugs or alcohol leads to lack of self-control. This is contrary to God's intentions for us. We must always be of sound mind and body to do the will of God in our lives.

- **Does this mean the Church says that one should never drink alcohol or use drugs?**

  Unless medically indicated, the Church prohibits the use of drugs. Alcohol is not prohibited but must be used only in moderation. One must never allow alcohol to take control of one's mind and body. The excessive use of alcohol and its ultimate addiction causes us to put alcohol before God since it becomes the primary focus of our lives. In effect, it replaces God.

- **Which Scripture passages are relevant to the issue of drugs and alcohol?**

  Old Testament

  Proverbs 20:1

  Proverbs 23:21

  Habakkuk 2 15–16

  New Testament

  John 2:1–11

  Ephesians 5:18

- **What can I do to counter drug and alcohol abuse in my school or community?**

  There are several things you can do to counter drug and alcohol use in your school or community. For example,

  1. Pray.
  2. Educate yourself on the issue so that you can inform and witness to friends and family.
  3. Find and develop alternatives to drinking and using drugs. Get others involved. Many communities, state governments, and the United States government have funding available to start such programs. Be creative. Ask your school or church to set up weekend night activities as drinking alternatives.
  4. Be a friend to those who you think have a drug or alcohol problem. Help them seek professional and/or spiritual help.

DRUGS & ALCOHOL DILEMMA #1

Alex and Jonathon grew up as neighbors, attended school together, and played on the same sports teams. During these years of grade school they were best friends. However, by the time they reached high school they began to make very different choices. Jonathon does well in school and generally stays out of trouble. He has experimented with alcohol on two occasions, but has never been drunk or used any kind of illegal drugs.

On the other hand, Alex has gained a reputation as a troublemaker. He spends a lot of time acting out in order to gain attention. Most of his weekends (and some weeknights) are spent getting drunk and high. Alex was also cited by the police for underage consumption, curfew violation, and driving without a license. Alex received warning that one more disciplinary incident at school or with the police will result in placement in a juvenile detention center.

Today, the high school held a series of random locker checks. With nothing to hide, Jonathon was not worried when called to the office. However, he discovered to his shock that his locker had been searched and a small amount of marijuana had been found. Jonathon knew what happened. Since Jonathon's locker is on the first floor, Alex often uses it to store books and supplies when in a hurry. Alex is the only person to whom Jonathon has given the combination. Jonathon has little doubt that Alex put the pot in his locker.

Given the very different reputations the boys have, Jonathon feels certain that if he explains the situation, his principal will give him the benefit of the doubt. The principal also know that Jonathon and Alex are friends.

Discussion Questions:

1) What choices does Jonathon have in this situation?

2) Make a list of the possible positive and negative affects that might result from each of Jonathon's decisions.

3) In what ways do you think Alex's choice will affect the boys' friendship?

4) In what ways do you think Jonathon's decision will effect the boys' friendship?

We have discussed this Tough Choice.

_____
Parent/Guardian Signature

_____
Student Signature

DRUGS & ALCOHOL DILEMMA #2

Courtney and Jenny are good friends. They are both juniors. Courtney is a varsity starter on the girls soccer team. The team is ranked first in the state and is headed to the playoffs. Jenny is a member of S.U.D.S. (Stop Underage Drinking among Students). She tries to raise awareness of the harmful effects that can result from alcohol consumption. The school which the girls attend has an official policy dealing with underage drinking. If students are discovered drinking alcohol, they are suspended and banned from extracurricular activities for one year. The policy has not deterred students from drinking. Due to the severity of the problem, the administration recently created a special alcohol task force. The principal asked Jenny if she would be a member, and Jenny agreed. Jenny will be one of a few students who act as "watchdogs" for the administration on the weekends. If students are seen drinking alcohol, Jenny will report their names to the administration.

Jenny attends a party celebrating the soccer team's success. One of the first things she sees upon entering the house is Courtney drinking with other members of the team. No other members of the task force are at the party.

Discussion Questions:

1) What should Jenny do?

2) Would it be right for Jenny to help Courtney out but not the others who are drinking?

3) How are the parents whose house is being used for the party responsible?

4) How could Jenny best be a "friend"?

We have discussed this Tough Choice.

_____   _____

Parent/Guardian Signature   Student Signature

DRUGS & ALCOHOL DILEMMA #3

It is the middle of basketball season and Joey has worked very hard. He is the first player off the bench and thinks there may be potential to become a starter before the end of the season. Joey has been competing with Vince for the starting position the entire season and feels that he may be close to earning that starting spot.

Yesterday Joey saw Vince smoking a cigarette behind the school building with some of his friends (none of whom are on the team). Joey knows that Vince regularly meets at this spot during his free period. Joey thinks that if he turns Vince in, he may get his spot as a starter. However, Joey also knows that Vince will probably be suspended from the team if the coach finds out.

Discussion Questions:

1) What should Joey do?

2) Would it matter if Vince was not a friend? Not a starter?

3) Would it matter if Joey did not agree with the school policy in the first place?

4) Should Joey discuss this with Vince first?

We have discussed this Tough Choice.

_____

Parent/Guardian Signature

_____

Student Signature

DRUGS & ALCOHOL DILEMMA #4

John's parents have specific rules that he is not only *not* to use drugs, but he is not to associate with anyone who does use drugs. This was agreed upon in a conversation several months ago. Recently, John befriended Charles, a new student at school, and invited him over to his house after school. John and Charles spend the afternoon watching a movie and playing computer games. After some time, Charles asks John if he wants to get high. When John says "no" Charles excuses himself, goes outside of the house, and smokes a joint by himself.

Discussion Questions:

1) What should John do?

2) What options does John have?

3) If John is sure his parents will never find out, would that change what John should do?

4) What is your view on drugs and people who use them?

5) How do drugs harm society?

We have discussed this Tough Choice.

_____   _____

Parent/Guardian Signature   Student Signature

DRUGS & ALCOHOL DILEMMA #5

Antoine's brother Jacob is twenty-two years old. One Saturday with their parents away, Antoine asks Jacob to buy him and his friends some beer for an upcoming party. Antoine tells Jacob that he will drink the beer at a friend's house and that he plans to spend the night there.

Discussion Questions:

1) What should Jacob do?

2) Does it matter that Antoine promised not to drive anywhere?

3) Would it matter if Jacob stayed home and supervised his brother's drinking?

4) Would Jacob be responsible if something were to happen to Antoine and his friends?

We have discussed this Tough Choice.

_____   _____

Parent/Guardian Signature   Student Signature

DRUGS & ALCOHOL DILEMMA #6

Laura, a senior in college, attends a party at an off campus apartment complex. At the party Laura has several alcoholic beverages and she is unable to drive home. However, she has friends at the party who have not had a drink who can take her home.

Laura begins to talk to a guy at the party named Bill who lives at the apartment. The first hour Laura talks to Bill she really feels comfortable and enjoys herself. However, as the evening progresses, Bill says some things that make Laura uneasy. Bill makes several inappropriate sexual advances toward Laura. Laura discovers that all of the designated drivers have left already. She wants to leave immediately to get away from Bill.

Discussion Questions:

1) Should Laura risk driving home in order to get away from Bill?

2) How might Laura get out of this situation without risking danger to herself or others?

3) How could this situation have been prevented?

We have discussed this Tough Choice.

_____

Parent/Guardian Signature

_____

Student Signature

DRUGS & ALCOHOL DILEMMA #7

Brandon's parents allow him to spend the night at his friend Tommy's house as long as he is ready to come home by 8:00 a.m. the next morning so the family will be on time for a trip to visit Brandon's grandmother. Brandon has an agreement with his parents not to attend unsupervised parties, especially ones where alcohol is served. Once at Tommy's, Brandon and Tommy decide to attend an unsupervised party in the adjacent town. Brandon has a few beers at the party knowing that Tommy has promised to be the designated driver.

At about midnight, Brandon notices Tommy holding a beer. He questions Tommy about this, but Tommy reassures him that he will only drink a couple to be sociable. At around 2:00 a.m., Brandon knows that he and Tommy need to be leaving. When he finds Tommy, he sees that Tommy still has a beer and appears to be slightly intoxicated. Both boys are too drunk to drive. Many others at the party are spending the night. But if Brandon does not meet his parents by 8 a.m. they will find out that he went to a party.

Discussion Questions:

1) What should Brandon do?

2) What options are open to Brandon?

3) When is punishment the better alternative to choose?

4) Is there a set limit to how many beers a person can have until they are "unfit" to drive?

We have discussed this Tough Choice.

_____

Parent/Guardian Signature

_____

Student Signature

DRUGS & ALCOHOL DILEMMA #8

Kalah is a freshman who made the varsity soccer team during recent tryouts. Through this experience, she has made a lot of new upperclassmen friends. This has greatly increased Kalah's popularity at school. The weekend before the team's first game, Kalah is invited to a party at one of the older girls' houses. She is told the party is "for soccer players only" so not to mention it to anyone else. Kalah goes to the party and has a great time as many of the older players act out skits that poke fun at the coaches and teachers of the school. After about an hour, the team captain announces that all the new varsity members need to sit in a circle. The five new members, including Kalah, do so. The captain then says it is time for the initiation to begin. The older players bring out some tequila and tell the new players to take "a few" shots in order to begin the initiation proceedings. Kalah is afraid to take part in this, but she wants to be accepted by the older girls.

Discussion Questions:

1) What should Kalah do?

2) How does social acceptance compare with individual integrity in your life?

3) Would it matter if the coach of the team had explicitly forbidden or condoned this activity?

4) What are ways Kalah could say "no" to the drinking and still be accepted?

5) Would acceptance be worth it in a situation like that?

We have discussed this Tough Choice.

_____   _____
Parent/Guardian Signature   Student Signature

Notes

1. Michael P. Dunlap, Psy.D, Clinical Psychologist at
   http://www.oregoncounseling.org/ArticlesPapers/Documents/ETOHBIOFx.htm

2. Ibid.

3. Gail Gleason Milgram, Ed.D. Rutgers University Center for Alcohol Studies, *The Effects of Alcohol*,   at http://www.rci.rutgers.edu/~cas2/fact15.shtml

4. Alcohol and drug information series number 1 for professionals. (Perth: The Drug Education Centre, West Australian Alcohol and Drug Authority: 1986.)

5. R. Breakspeare and Starmer G. Breakspeare, *The Art of Sensible Drinking,* (Sydney: Ellsyd Press; 1986).

6. Gail Gleason Milgram, Ed.D. at http://www.rci.rutgers.edu/~cas2/fact15.shtml

7. *The National Household Survey of Drug Abuse (NHSDA) Report*, published by the Office of Applied Studies, Substance Abuse and Mental Health Services Administration (SAMHSA) of the U.S. Department of Health and Human Services (2002).

8. SAMHSA Fact Sheet—Consequences of Underage Alcohol Use at http://www.health.org/govpubs/rpo992/

9. B.F. Grant, "The impact of a family history of alcoholism on the relationship between age at onset of alcohol use and DSM-IV alcohol dependence: Results from the National Longitudinal Alcohol Epidemiologic Survey," *Alcohol Health and Research World*, 22 (1998).

10. National Institute of Alcohol Abuse and Alcoholism, *Alcohol Health and Research World*, 17, no. 2, (1993).

11. Office of the Inspector General, Report to the Surgeon General, *Youth and Alcohol: Dangerous and Deadly Consequences* (Washington, D.C.: U.S. Department of Education, 1992).

12. National Institute of Alcohol Abuse and Alcoholism, "Youth Drinking: Risk Factors and Consequences," *Alcohol Alert* no. 37 (July 1997).

13. H.S. Swartzwelder, W.A. Wilson, and M.I. Tayyeb, "Age-dependent inhibition of long-term potentiation by ethanol in immature versus mature hippocampus," *Alcoholism: Clinical Experimental Research*, vol. 20, (1996).

14. National Center on Addiction and Substance Abuse, *Rethinking Rites of Passage: Substance Abuse on America's Campuses*, (New York: Columbia University, 1994).

15. National Institute on Drug Abuse, *National Survey Results on Drug Use from The Monitoring the Future Study, 1975–1997, Volume I: Secondary School Students* (Rockville, MD: Department of Health and Human Services, 1998).

16. *Rethinking Rites of Passage: Substance Abuse on America's Campuse*s.

17. National Highway Traffic Safety Administration, *Young Drivers Traffic Safety Facts 1997,* (Washington, D.C.: U.S. Department of Transportation, 1997).

18. Office of the Inspector General, Report to the Surgeon General, *Youth and Alcohol: Dangerous and Deadly Consequences,* (Washington, D.C.: U.S. Department of Education, 1992).

19. *Rethinking Rites of Passage: Substance Abuse on America's Campuses.*

20. American Lung Association, *State of the Air Report—June 2002*, Adolescent Smoking Statistics at www.lungusa.org/press/tobacco/not_stats.html

21. Ibid.

22. Ibid.

23. Ibid.

24. Centers for Disease Control and Prevention. *Preventing tobacco use among youth people: A report of the surgeon general.* (Atlanta, Georgia: CDC, 1994).

25. George H. Gallup International Institute. *Teenage attitudes and behavior concerning tobacco: report of the findings.* (Princeton, NJ: George H. Gallup International Institute, 1992).

26. Gary Huber, *Pharmacology Biochemistry and Behavior*, vol. 40. (1991).

27. M.S. Gold *Marijuana*, (New York: Plenum Medical Book Co.,1989): 227.

28. http://www.girlpower.gov/girlarea/bodyfx/marijuana.htm

29. R.H. Schwartz *Pediatric Clinics of North America* 34 (1987): 305–317.

30. Ibid.

31. S. Andreasson. et al., *Lancet* 2 (1987): 1483–1485.

32. M.S. Gold *Marijuana*, 69–71.

33. B. Zuckerman et al. *New England Journal of Medicine* 320 (1989): 762–768.

34. H.D. Kleber *Journal of Clinical Psychology* 49, no. 2(Supplement), (1988): 3–6.

35. http://www.nida.nih.gov/MarijBroch/Marijparentstxt.html

EATING DISORDERS
EATING DISORDERS
EATING DISORDERS
EATING DISORDERS
EATING DISORDERS
EATING DISORDERS

EATING DISORDERS

EATING DISORDERS
EATING DISORDERS
EATING DISORDERS
EATING DISORDERS
EATING DISORDERS
EATING DISORDERS
EATING DISORDERS
EATING DISORDERS
EATING DISORDERS
EATING DISORDERS
EATING DISORDERS
EATING DISORDERS
EATING DISORDERS
EATING DISORDERS
EATING DISORDERS
EATING DISORDERS

Overview of Eating Disorder Issues • • • • •

- **What are eating disorders?**

Eating disorders are disturbing eating behaviors or patterns of using food for emotional reasons. While the frequency, severity, and causes of these personal problems differ, the one thing they all have in common is the use of food as a way to cope with life. One thing that is typically not understood is that eating disorders are not just about food or being thin. Rather, they are part of an emotional system that affects every aspect of a sufferer's life. The main eating disorders are anorexia, bulimia, compulsive overeating, and chronic dieting. Most people with eating disorders are females, about 90 percent.[1]

- **What is anorexia? How is it harmful?**

Anorexics are typically perfectionists, and teenage anorexics tend to be high achievers in school. However, at the same time these individuals suffer from a very low self-esteem. Many feel that they are worthless or undeserving, although they may appear happy to outsiders. Needing some sense of mastery in life, an anorexic will experience a sense of control by saying no to the normal food demands of the body. This sense of control extends to other areas in life, including hours of sleep and amount of exercise a person will allow themselves to have.

Anorexics may also suffer in a number of physical ways from their disorder. They may experience hair loss, lowered body temperature, low blood pressure, lowered breathing rate, poor circulation, cessation of menstruation, diminished activity of the thyroid gland, lightheadedness, joint swelling, dry skin, brittle nails, insomnia, and an imbalance of body chemicals that can lead to heart failure.[2] It is important that anorexia is treated early because as the disorder becomes more entrenched, the damage that it does becomes less reversible.

- **What is bulimia? How is it harmful?**

Bulimia nervosa involves the combination of episodic eating of large quantities of food (binging) and then getting rid of the food by vomiting or using laxatives or diuretics (purging). Unlike anorexics, whose extreme weight loss is apparent, bulimics may appear to maintain an average weight, making their disorder more difficult to detect.

Like anorexics, bulimics are often perfectionists at whatever they do, yet suffer from very low self-esteem and even depression. Bulimics often display other compulsive behaviors, such as shoplifting or alcohol abuse. While normal food intake for women and teenagers is 2,000 to 3,000 calories a day, one study suggested that bulimics binge an average of 3,400 calories in a 75 minute span.[3] After purging their system, bulimics often fast or exercise excessively for large periods of the day.

Bulimia has serious health consequences. Purging upsets the body's electrolyte balance for chemicals such as sodium, potassium, and calcium. This results in fatigue, seizures, irregular heartbeat, and bone thinning. The act of constant purging can affect the body's organs, as well. Stomach acid brought up through purging can damage the esophagus and stomach, cause gums to recede, erode tooth enamel, and scar or bruise fingers.[4]

- **What is compulsive overeating? How is it harmful?**

Individuals who binge on food but do not purge are compulsive overeaters. Not everyone who eats a lot of food falls into this category. Most sufferers of this disorder eat when they are not hungry and continue to eat until after they are full. Compulsive overeaters use food for emotional rather than nutritional reasons. Turning to food may be a way to seek comfort when stressed, to rebel against stereotypical roles in society, or to swallow hurtful feelings such as anger.

While it is not a necessary characteristic of a binge eating disorder, most people who suffer from this illness are either obese or have a genetic predisposition to weigh more than average. Obesity occurs when the body has too many fat cells, the fat cells are too large, or there is a combination of both. Most people of average weight have around 30 billion fat cells in their bodies. Obese people typically have between 100 and 200 billion fat cells.[5] When an individual accumulates that many fat cells, he or she will always have difficulty maintaining a healthy weight. While a high calorie diet, lack of exercise, and genetics all play roles in causing obesity, it is not known what triggers a compulsive eating disorder. Certain experts suggest that there may be some connection to depression.

The behaviors and health risks to binge eating disorder and obesity are many. Typically, victims of a binge eating disorder will eat faster than usual, eat in privacy, not be able to control how much they eat, and will feel guilty or self-hatred after eating. The health complications that could result if treatment is not sought out are: heart disease, high blood pressure, high cholesterol, diabetes, gallbladder disease, various types of cancer, sleep apnea, joint pain, depression, and death.[6]

- **What is chronic dieting? How is it harmful?**

Chronic dieting is the constant need for certain individuals to be on a diet. It is caused by an unnecessarily compulsive pursuit of thinness, dissatisfaction with body shape, preoccupation with food, and fear of becoming fat. Chronic dieting upsets normal eating behaviors. It is usually accompanied by feelings of failure and renewed promises to diet.

Often, chronic dieters will switch from diet to diet, but will come away feeling unsuccessful from each one. Chronic dieting may be accompanied by excessive exercising, negative self-images, and avoidance of social situations. Chronic dieting is harmful because it leads to nutritional deficiency, resulting in many of the same problems facing anorexics. Psychologically, chronic dieters' self-esteem is tied to their physical appearance. Their constant unhappiness with weight leads to periodic and long-term depression.

- **How many people are affected by eating disorders?**

The national Association of Anorexia Nervosa and Associated Disorders (ANAD) found that eating disorders affect seven million women and one million men.[7] From the study, 86 percent of those affected reported that the onset of their illness took place before the age of 20.[8] In terms of duration, 77 percent reported that their illness lasted between one and fifteen years.[9] A 1990 study found that 11 percent of high-school students suffered from bulimia or anorexia, with that number rising by the year.[10] A major problem is that many people with eating disorders do not seek professional treatment. The longer someone goes without treatment, the less likely they are to recover and more likely they are to damage their bodies permanently. Without treatment, up to 20 percent of those with eating disorders die, while that number falls to two to three percent with treatment.[11] About 60 percent of individuals who seek treatment recover.[12]

- **What should a person do if he or she suspects a friend has an eating disorder?**

Above all else, remain a friend who is sincere, supportive, and caring. Let the friend know of the concern and encourage the person with the eating disorder to obtain professional help. However, do not try to analyze the problems, nor assume responsibility for altering the eating behaviors. Contact a counselor for additional recommendations.

It is important to know that eating disorders can be treated, but only by professionals. Treatment usually involves medical, nutritional, and psychological evaluations, counseling, and therapy. The length of treatment depends upon the cause and duration of the eating disorder. The sooner a person with an eating disorder seeks help, the sooner he or she can recover. Since the rate of reoccurance is high in eating disorders, a person may require treatment for life.

Church Teaching on Eating Disorders • • • • •

- **What is the Church's teaching on eating disorders?**

The Church does not specifically address "eating disorders," but it does address high-risk behaviors, especially among teenagers. The United States Catholic bishops wrote:[13]

> Special attention should be given to young people who engage in high-risk behaviors that endanger their own health and well-being. These young people often have multiple problems that can severely limit their futures—fragmented family life, poor school performance, antisocial behavior, *eating disorders*, sexual activity, sexual confusion as they struggle with identity, and alcohol or drug use, to name several. The Church is called to work with the wider community to address the needs of these young people. Ministry to these young people may be the most important way they will ever come to know and feel the love of God—through people who love them and care for them just at the point when they themselves feel least worthy and lovable.

- **Why is that the teaching of the Catholic Church?**

The virtue of temperance calls for control of all types of abuse, including food. Also the fifth commandment ("Thou shall not kill") calls on us to care for our bodies, not abuse them.

- **Which Scripture passages are relevant to the issue of eating disorders?**

Genesis 1:27

I Corinthians 6:19–20

EATING DISORDER DILEMMA #1

Jill and Stacey have been good friends throughout high school. After Christmas break, they both decide to diet and exercise. They begin to watch what they eat and work out together. By the end of February, both girls are excited to see the results. Over the next month however, Jill notices that Stacey keeps getting thinner. Jill doesn't think much of this at first, but she begins to notice little things, such as Stacey throwing away her lunch and increasing her workouts to two hours a day. Jill becomes concerned and asks Stacey if maybe she is losing too much weight. Stacey laughs her off and tells Jill not to worry, that she is "only getting in shape for prom." A few weeks before prom, Jill notices how Stacey's clothes seem to hang on her and that Stacey seems much more withdrawn than usual. Jill again brings up the issue of weight loss, but Stacey gets angry saying, "I thought you were my friend." When Jill says she feels Stacey might need to talk to somebody about this, Stacey insists that such a move would ultimately end their friendship. Jill isn't sure if Stacey is anorexic or not. She is worried about losing her as a friend.

Discussion Questions:

1) What should Jill do?

2) What does "being a good friend" mean?

3) Is having a friend be angry with you sometimes okay?

4) To whom can Jill turn for help?

We have discussed this Tough Choice.

_____   _____

Parent/Guardian Signature   Student Signature

EATING DISORDER DILEMMA #2

Craig and Dave are very good friends. They enjoy hanging out at the local pizza parlor with other kids from school. A few months ago, Craig left the table immediately after a meal to go to the bathroom. When he came back, someone joked that they suspected Craig was bulimic. Everyone, including Craig, laughed because Craig is a muscular guy who is very outgoing, healthy, and active in sports. Dave didn't think much more about the incident.

Then, last week, Craig had a seizure at football practice. When talking to one of his teammates, Dave found out that this wasn't the first time such an episode had happened. It led Dave to observe Craig more closely. He noticed how Craig fell asleep in class and how he typically left the lunchroom to go use the rest room in the locker area.

When Dave goes to Craig's house to pick him up on this Friday night, nobody answers the door. Dave walks into the living room and discovers Craig on the floor. He is conscious, but he is having trouble getting up. When Dave asks Craig if he should call the paramedics, Craig gets upset and says, "No! I'm fine…just got a little light headed."

Discussion Questions:

1) What should Dave do?

2) Is it surprising to find that males also have eating disorders?

3) Is it possible to have an eating disorder yet appear healthy-looking?

4) What causes eating disorders?

5) What can be done for those with eating disorders?

We have discussed this Tough Choice.

_____

Parent/Guardian Signature

_____

Student Signature

EATING DISORDER DILEMMA #3

Rachel has been overweight her entire life. Because most of her family is also overweight, she never used to think much about it. But ever since she entered high school, she has begun to feel a bit more uncomfortable about her body. She is interested in guys, but she feels that nobody will be interested in her because she is heavy. To make matters worse, whenever she feels particularly depressed, she will eat a large quantity of food to "feel better."

This week is especially trying on Rachel, as homecoming is near and nobody has asked her to the dance. Rachel's friend, Brittany, knows that Rachel is feeling stressed. She also knows that Rachel uses food to soothe her emotions, but the two have never talked about it. Brittany sees Rachel in the hallway the day before the dance and notices Rachel crying. When Brittany asks her what is wrong, Rachel indicates that she doesn't feel well and is going to check out of school to go home.

Discussion Questions:

1) What should Brittany do?

2) What is the danger of using food for emotional reasons?

3) How valuable is physical appearance to you compared to the rest of the person? Why?

4) Are you happy with your physical appearance? Why or why not?

We have discussed this Tough Choice.

_____   _____

Parent/Guardian Signature   Student Signature

Notes

1. Anorexia Nervosa and Related Eating Disorders (ANRED), Inc., Eating Disorder Statistics, February 2002, at http://www.anred.com/stats.html

2. http://www.eating-disorder.org/anorexia.html

3. Dixie Farley. "On the Teen Scene: Eating Disorders Require Medical Attention." U.S. Food and Drug Administration, FDA Consumer magazine (March 1992, revised September 1997). Also at http://stress.about.com/library/blteeneatingdis.htm

4. Ibid.

5. http://www.eating-disorder.org/obesity.html

6. http://www.eating-disorder.org/binge_eating.html

7. National Association of Anorexia Nervosa and Associated Disorders (ANAD), Facts about Eating Disorders at http://www.anad.org/facts.htm

8. Ibid.

9. Ibid.

10. National Association of Anorexia Nervosa and Associated Disorders (ANAD), High School Study of Eating Disorders, at http://www.anad.org/hsstudy.htm

11. Anorexia Nervosa and Related Eating Disorders (ANRED), Inc., Eating Disorder Statistics, February 2002, at http://www.anred.com/stats.html

12. Ibid.

13. United States Catholic Bishops. "Renewing the Vision: A Framework for Catholic Youth Ministry."

EUTHANASIA
EUTHANASIA
EUTHANASIA
EUTHANASIA
EUTHANASIA
EUTHANASIA

EUTHANASIA

EUTHANASIA
EUTHANASIA
EUTHANASIA
EUTHANASIA
EUTHANASIA
EUTHANASIA
EUTHANASIA
EUTHANASIA
EUTHANASIA
EUTHANASIA
EUTHANASIA
EUTHANASIA
EUTHANASIA
EUTHANASIA
EUTHANASIA

Overview of Euthanasia Issues • • • • • • • •

- ## What is euthanasia?

Euthanasia translates roughly from Greek to mean "good death" or "easy death". Euthanasia is the killing of one person by another to relieve the suffering of that person. It is also known erroneously as "mercy killing".

- ## What are some other terms associated with euthanasia issues?

There are many other relevant terms related to euthanasia. *Active euthanasia* involves taking deliberate action to end the life of a dying or suffering individual. *Passive euthanasia* is a term meaning the disconnecting of life support equipment or other life-sustaining medical treatments to allow the natural death of the patient to occur. Passive euthanasia is in fact not euthanasia at all but is better expressed by the phrase "letting die". *Assisted suicide* deals with providing the means (drugs, etc.) by which a person can end his or her own life. *Physician-assisted suicide* occurs when a doctor provides the drugs which will end a person's life. *Terminal illness* is a condition suffered by a sick person for which there is no known cure. *Living will* is the name given to an individual's legal document informing a physician not to connect or to disconnect life-support equipment if such an action would simply delay an inevitable death. *DNR* (Do not resuscitate) is the order on a patient's medical charts informing doctors that no extraordinary measures should be taken to save the patient's life. *CPR* (Cardiopulmonary resuscitation) is the procedure done in order to get a patient's heart to begin beating again. This will automatically be done should the heart stop, unless there is a DNR order. *Palliative care* is care involving no extraneous means of keeping an individual alive. Persons are simply offered hydration and comfort.

- ## Is euthanasia legal?

Euthanasia is generally outlawed around the world. Although some countries do not specifically have laws against it, other laws or national traditions make it very clear that it is illegal. In fact, only Switzerland, Belgium, and the Netherlands legally allow physician-assisted suicides. In the United States, Oregon's law permits physician-assisted suicide for the terminally ill under limited circumstances. Since its implementation in 1997, over 100 terminally ill people have taken advantage of that law to end their lives. Several states and Congress are considering changes to make euthanasia legal.

- ## How many people die from physician-assisted suicides in the United States?

It is unknown how many physician-assisted deaths occur in the United States. Due to the laws preventing assisted suicide, anyone who practices it risks prosecution. A Michigan physician, Dr. Jack Kevorkian, M.D., claims to have assisted in the death of at least 130 people, according to a report on the finalexit.org website. While these numbers cannot be confirmed, Kevorkian was convicted of second degree murder and use of a controlled substance in a 1999 Michigan case. He is currently serving a ten to twenty-five year term for the murder charge and a concurrent three to seven year term for the substance charge.

- ## Are there any national laws or Supreme Court cases dealing with euthanasia?

In 1997, President Bill Clinton signed the Federal Assisted Suicide Funding Restriction Act, which prohibits the use of federal funds to support physician-assisted suicide. While there are other Supreme Court cases, two that speak to our government's position on physician-assisted suicides are the following:

> *Vacco v. Quill* (1997). In this case, New York physicians and three terminally ill patients sued the State's Attorney General on the grounds that the New York law against assisted suicide violated the Equal Protection Clause of the Fourteenth Amendment to the United States Constitution. The Supreme Court stated that New York neither infringed upon

individuals' fundamental rights nor treated anyone differently in drawing distinctions between people. It concluded that while "everyone, regardless of physical condition, is entitled, if competent, to refuse unwanted lifesaving medical treatment; no one is permitted to assist a suicide."

Washington v. Glucksberg (1997). Four Washington physicians and three ill patients sued the State of Washington and its Attorney General, claiming the State's law preventing assisted suicide was unconstitutional, because it violated the Due Process Clause of the Fourteenth Amendment to the United States Constitution. The Supreme Court decided that a person's "right" to assistance in committing suicide was not a fundamental liberty whose interest was protected in the Due Process Clause. The Court uses two criteria when deciding if an action violates the Due Process Clause: 1) the Clause protects rights and liberties that are deeply rooted in our nation's history and tradition, and 2) the Court requires a "careful description" of the fundamental liberty that is being violated. The Court said that the "liberty to choose a humane, dignified death" and other descriptors did not fulfill the second criterion, and that no place existed in our country's traditions where this right could be found.

- **What are the main arguments *for* and *against* euthanasia?**
  1. A person should have the right to eliminate pain and choose to end their own life.

Argument: Cases wherein euthanasia is debated involve individuals who are experiencing pain and suffering and whose activities of daily living are limited due to the disease process. Many times, these people are completely dependent upon their families for day-to-day care. Allowing these people to end their lives would relieve them of the remainder of a life in constant pain, with minimal quality, and which places a heavy burden on their family.

Response: There are no absolute criteria by which to judge quality of a life. Each life is inherently good in and of itself. It is up to the individual to seek out the good of life while this precious gift is still available to that person. Since God is the One who gave the gift of life, only God can determine when that life has concluded its purpose. To legalize the deliberate killing of human beings fundamentally undermines the basis of law and morality. Counseling and medical intervention can help individuals through pain and suffering. Given the instructional power associated with suffering, the individual and persons surrounding him or her often discover qualities and lessons which may otherwise have gone unnoticed. Families and loved ones exist to celebrate with individuals in good times and support them during bad times. True loved ones are never a burden.

  2. A person should have the right to die with dignity.

Argument: Many times, the people in question are going through a horrific experience. Not only are they facing the prospect of death from a terminal illness, but they may have physical or mental problems which decrease the amount of dignity with which they can carry out their lives. People who plead for euthanasia may suffer from an inability to control their bowel function, painful sores, constant headaches, blindness, lack of muscle coordination, Alzheimer's disease, decreased brain function and altered mobility due to a stroke, or many other debilitating conditions. They should be allowed to die when they are prepared to do so.

Response: Once again, each life is precious, and each life allows the individual to do some good for others. Dignity is a very subjective term, open to much interpretation. In cases like these, dignity more frequently reflects personal pride. While discomfort and disfigurement often accompany these conditions and normal coping skills are stressed, life is not without value.

3. Euthanasia is a financially intelligent option. It will save money that could have been spent on long-term medical care.

Argument: The costs of medical care impose tremendous economic burdens on the families of terminally ill patients. Euthanasia is a way to eliminate the massive bills incurred by patients in the last weeks and months of their lives. Since it is a foregone conclusion that life ends, individuals and families should be allowed to end their own or a loved one's life in a way that places the least amount of burden on both the patient and his or her family. Money spent on palliative care could be used elsewhere, both for the families and for the health care providers.

Response: To say that financial gain should take precedence over the longevity of an individual's life means that the money has more value than human life. It is erroneous to assume money would be saved if euthanasia would be legalized. Financial support for appropriate geriatric and palliative care would be decreased. Ultimately, those needing such services, the elderly, the terminally ill, and the disenfranchised, might not be able to afford any care. Research funding could be eliminated, and as people continue to age euthanasia might be forcibly encouraged.

4. Having available the option of euthanasia will decrease the pressure placed on those who are terminally ill.

Argument: Those who are ill are acting for the betterment of others when they choose assisted suicide. Many times it is out of the love for family members or loved ones that they choose to alleviate the burden on their loved ones. They can die peacefully and in good conscience, knowing that they have made their families' lives a little easier.

Also, legalizing euthanasia would free patients of concern that their actions would get the physicians who are assisting them in trouble. While they may want to end their lives, patients may hesitate due to the legal issues likely to be experienced by those assisting them.

Response: This argument is without merit. Legalizing euthanasia increases the pressure placed on terminally ill patients and undermines many of the realities of life and death that currently exist.

Having the option of euthanasia gives rise to new pressures placed on vulnerable patients to volunteer. This results in much stress and suffering. Patients who want to avoid being a burden to their families and take the honorable route in ending their lives, might seriously alter family relationships. Such a decision could undermine trust between doctors and patients. Having euthanasia as an available option, patients and families may be uncertain about the health care practitioners' diagnosis and potentially ill-advised treatments. Doctors and health care providers might decide matters based on what they felt best for their patients—a cruel and final act of medical paternalism.

5. Euthanasia is easily controlled through the legislative process and safer than allowing uncertified health care professionals to assist suicide in the manner most convenient for the practitioner.

Argument: When laws are passed and guidelines or rules are instituted, euthanasia would be permitted. The current system encourages individuals interested in euthanasia to seek practitioners with neither the training nor the access to proper medical equipment. Legalization allows the process to be monitored in hospitals, not in the backs of vans.

Response: A system which legalizes euthanasia would be nearly impossible to regulate. It would lead to a variety of different procedures. Each state would need to determine how to implement a euthanasia policy. Attempting to come up with an infrastructure to oversee the patients, methods, and physicians would require huge amounts of money and would guarantee neither quality nor control.

Lawmakers would determine life and death decision-making of those most likely to be affected by euthanasia—the elderly, the terminally ill, and the disenfranchised. The people who apply those laws—

the medical care providers—would make judgments on the lives of the same groups of people. However, those affected by such legislation have no power to draft *or* execute the law. This reasoning ties into the "slippery-slope" argument in the final response.

6. Euthanasia is a simple decision affecting the life of one individual.

Argument: It is each individual's right to decide how to live or end his or her life. Legalizing euthanasia would simply allow this process to continue. If an individual believes that he or she has a reason to end his or her life, the government should protect and help facilitate that right.

Response: Legalizing euthanasia is dangerous because death is irreversible. Many people suffer from either clinical depression, are uninformed about the meaning of their diagnosis, or are misdiagnosed. In such cases, while the will to end one's life might be present, the reasoning is not. Allowing assisted suicide would close the doors to those individuals who might be helped—even cured—by alternative methods.

The main danger of legalizing euthanasia is that it creates a slippery-slope, in judging the value of human life and the individuals making this judgment. Holding the opinion that all human life is sacred implicitly states that no human life is more worthy than another. But in making exceptions in legalizing which lives can be ended designates that some lives are more worth living than others. Proceeding on this road is very dangerous because of potential ramifications. If the elderly or terminally ill are able to be legally killed, why not the mentally handicapped? What about the blind and lame? Or perhaps certain infants? Those who think this is an unrealistic possibility need only look to Nazi Germany, where instances of legalizing voluntary euthanasia led to the legalization of involuntary euthanasia. No system created could ever be foolproof once the initial steps were taken, even with very stringent guidelines.

Church Teaching on Euthanasia • • • • • • • • •

- **What is the Catholic Church's position on euthanasia?**

  The Catholic Church is unequivocally against the practice of euthanasia. It considers it the equivalent of murder. The *Catechism of the Catholic Church* states: "Whatever its motives and means, direct euthanasia consists in putting an end to the lives of handicapped, sick, or dying persons. It is morally unacceptable" (2277).

- **Why is that the position of the Catholic Church?**

  The *Catechism* also explains: "Those whose lives are diminished or weakened deserve special respect. Sick or handicapped persons should be helped to lead lives as normal as possible." All people deserve respect and dignity.

- **What else does the Church say about euthanasia?**

  Pope John Paul II wrote in his encyclical *The Gospel of Life*:

  > We see a tragic expression of all this [people trying to control their lives too much] in the spread of *euthanasia*—disguised and surreptitious, or practiced openly and even legally. As well as for reasons of a misguided pity at the sight of the patient's suffering, euthanasia is sometimes justified by the utilitarian motive of avoiding costs which bring no return and which weigh heavily on society. Thus it is proposed to eliminate malformed babies, the severely handicapped, the disabled, the elderly, especially when they are not self-sufficient, and the terminally ill. Nor can we remain silent in the face of other more furtive, but no less serious and real, forms of euthanasia. These could occur for example when, in order to increase the availability of organs for transplants, organs are removed without respecting objective and adequate criteria which verify the death of the donor.

- **Which Scripture passages are relevant to the euthanasia issue?**

  Exodus 20:12

  Ruth 4:13–26

  Job 12:12

  Psalms 148:12–13

  Proverbs 23:22

- **What should I do to show my opposition for euthanasia?**

  There are many ways to oppose euthanasia. They include:

  1. Involving yourself politically. This could mean writing and meeting your elected representatives at the local, state, and federal levels. This could also mean running for office yourself.
  2. Starting a Pro-life club at your school or in your church.
  3. Talking about the issues with your parents and loved ones.

EUTHANASIA DILEMMA #1

Shelby had never liked hospitals, and today was no exception. She made her way to room 201 without making a sound. As she entered, she saw the inert form of her grandfather lying in bed. Shelby's grandfather recently had a severe stroke. He had been in a coma and on life support for a week. The doctors gave him almost no chance to regain consciousness. They said he would need to be on life support for the rest of his life. Shelby's parents had talked with her and mentioned the option of taking him off life support. Shelby had heard of euthanasia, but had never thought she would have to deal with it on a first-hand basis. She knew euthanasia was against Church teaching. Her family wanted her input on the matter. She knew that she loved her grandfather, and did not want to see him die. She also knew that she didn't want him to suffer either.

Discussion Questions:

1) What do you think Shelby should say?

2) Why do you think the Church is against euthanasia?

3) Is it ever justifiable to take or end a life?

4) Whose pain is eased by euthanasia: the patient's or the family's?

We have discussed this Tough Choice.

_____   _____

Parent/Guardian Signature   Student Signature

EUTHANASIA DILEMMA #2

Tom was on his deathbed. The cancer had now spread from his lungs to his brain. In addition to severe breathing difficulties, Tom now experienced almost complete speech and memory loss, muscle spasms, lack of bowel control—and intense and constant pain. He no longer recognized Helen, his wife of fifty years, and a registered nurse. Doctors estimated that he had less than six weeks to live.

Markelle was Tom's chief doctor. It was difficult for her to witness the change in Tom from a happy and vibrant man to his current vegetative and hopeless state. Meanwhile, Helen wanted Tom to be at peace and out of his suffering.

One afternoon, Helen approached Markelle and pleaded for help. She asked Markelle if there was anything that could be done to end Tom's suffering and speed up his death. Markelle explained that while Tom had a "living will" that stipulated that no extensive measures should be taken to keep him alive, as a doctor, there was nothing she could actively do to end Tom's life.

Helen cried and asked the doctor if she could get a prescription of morphine for her own pain. Markelle had little doubt Helen planned to administer the medication to Tom. Both were aware that even a small amount extra of morphine would most certainly bring a quick end to Tom's life. Markelle understood that she would have no legal responsibility if Tom were to die this way.

Discussion Questions:

1) What should Markelle do?

2) What is her responsibility as a doctor?

3) Is there a difference between legal responsibility and moral responsibility? How so?

4) Is actively causing death the same as allowing someone to die without taking measures to prevent death?

5) Is there value in suffering? If so, what is the value?

We have discussed this Tough Choice.

_____

Parent/Guardian Signature

_____

Student Signature

HOMOSEXUALITY
HOMOSEXUALITY
HOMOSEXUALITY
HOMOSEXUALITY
HOMOSEXUALITY
HOMOSEXUALITY

HOMOSEXUALITY

HOMOSEXUALITY
HOMOSEXUALITY
HOMOSEXUALITY
HOMOSEXUALITY
HOMOSEXUALITY
HOMOSEXUALITY
HOMOSEXUALITY
HOMOSEXUALITY
HOMOSEXUALITY
HOMOSEXUALITY
HOMOSEXUALITY
HOMOSEXUALITY
HOMOSEXUALITY
HOMOSEXUALITY
HOMOSEXUALITY
HOMOSEXUALITY

Overview of Homosexuality Issues • • • • • • •

- **What is sexual orientation?**

  Sexual orientation is a term referring to an individual's emotional, romantic, or sexual attraction to someone of a particular gender (male or female).

- **What are the types of sexual orientation?**

  Typically, there are three types of sexual orientation: *heterosexual orientation* (an attraction to a person of the opposite sex), *bisexual orientation* (an attraction to individuals of both sexes), and *homosexual orientation* (an attraction to individuals of one's own sex).

- **What does it mean to be homosexual?**

  Homosexuality is influenced by several different factors including feelings, behavior, and identity.[1] On the feelings level, individuals have a sexual attraction towards other people of the same sex. The behavioral level refers to individuals engaging in sexual behavior with people of the same sex. What is meant by the identity level is individuals describe themselves as being homosexual. It is important to understand the distinction between these different levels in order to try to make sense of the definition of homosexuality. Some people are attracted to members of the same sex but do not act on it. Some individuals engage in sexual behavior with members of the same sex but are more attracted to members of the opposite sex. Others feel an attraction to members of the same sex but do not think of themselves as homosexual. One or more of these categories can change over time, making it difficult to label someone as homosexual. But recognizing the distinction is important in shaping the picture of homosexuality in society and in regards to the Catholic Church's teaching.

- **Why are some people homosexual or bisexual?**

  It is very difficult to answer why some individuals are homosexual or bisexual because no definitive answer has been agreed upon. Some argue that such an attraction is genetic, that certain individuals are born with an orientation towards members of the same sex. Others say that societal factors, such as upbringing, influence the orientation. Still others believe it is a combination of both. A majority of scientists today agree that a person's sexual orientation results from environmental, biological, emotional, and societal factors. These factors may act differently for different individuals, but it is generally agreed upon that there is no single cause for all homosexual people.

- **When does a person think or know that he or she is homosexual? Is it a phase?**

  Again, there are no definitive answers as to when someone thinks he or she is homosexual. Homosexuality manifests itself at different times in different people. For some people it is a phase, for others it lasts throughout their lives. Some evidence points to the fact that homosexual experiences may be part of a transitional or experimental phase during youth.[2] When considering that adolescence is a time when many beliefs, identities, and authorities are questioned, this makes sense. Couple this with the fact that there may be some contributing family experiences, such as a female dominated upbringing or the absence of a male role model in a homosexual man's past, and it is easy to see how the confluence of factors could cause an individual to question everything about themselves.

  Other evidence shows that many adolescents are confused about their sexuality, but that many will turn out to be heterosexual.[3] At age twelve, 25.9 percent of children were unsure of their sexual orientation, compared to five percent who were uncertain at age seventeen. Of those who are sure about their sexuality, there are still some inconsistencies in regards to attraction, behavior, and identity: 95.5 percent of boys and 94.3 percent of girls said they were exclusively or primarily attracted to members of the opposite sex; 97.8 percent of boys and 96.9 percent of girls indicated that their fantasies were heterosexual; and 98.5 percent of boys and 98.9 percent of girls considered themselves to be heterosexual. This lack of consistency reveals that the developing sexual identity that takes place during the adolescent years may reveal fluid state of human sexuality.

- ## How many homosexual people are there?

A study conducted by Alfred Kinsey in the 1940s and 1950s revealed that roughly 10 percent of all men and a slightly lesser percentage of all women were homosexual. This study, although often used as a reference, has been widely criticized. As mentioned before, part of the difficulty in arriving at accurate measurements of the true number of homosexual people stems from the distinction between homosexual feelings, behavior, and identity. There are too many variables included to get an accurate definition of homosexuality, much less calculate numbers for that definition. Combined with the knowledge that sexuality is a fluid development that may change over time, it is very difficult to estimate exact numbers, though they are likely substantially less.

- ## What is homophobia?

Homophobia is a fear of and/or hostility towards homosexual individuals. People who exhibit this fear or hostility are often called homophobic. Sometimes homophobia is verbal and other times it can be violent. According to the FBI's Hate Crime Statistics, 17 percent of the 8,049 hate crimes in 1997 resulted from hostility to certain individuals' sexual orientation.[4]

Interestingly, this prejudice against homosexual people is more often exhibited by young males than young females.[5] The reasoning for this is that the boundaries on gender roles for boys are much more rigid than those for girls. Boys have a limited number of ways to express their emotions within their peer group. Therefore, any affection or expression between young males is often seen by peers as being homosexual. The friendships of young women, however, often involve emotional and physical signs of affection. Therefore, young women are less likely to be viewed by their peer group as having homosexual interest.

- ## What is meant by "coming out"?

"Coming out" refers to the complex process in which homosexual individuals reveal to other people that they are, in fact, homosexual. Because homophobia can affect a person's social relationships, self-esteem, and schoolwork, declaring sexual orientation is a very difficult thing to do.

Usually, coming out involves four steps.[6] *Sensitization* describes the time when a person begins to feel different from other people of the same sex. They may recognize a lack of interest in members of the opposite sex, but more likely they just acknowledge that their interests are different than what is generally supposed to be appropriate for their gender. This stage is followed by a *confusion of identity* involving more alternative perceptions, experiencing sexual arousal, recognition of social stigmas surrounding homosexuality, and realization that personal knowledge of homosexuality is lacking. Then an individual *assumes a homosexual identity*. In this stage, an individual begins to accept their homosexuality and express it in a positive way. *Commitment* involves openly proclaiming one's homosexuality.

- ## What are the dangers associated with homosexual sex?

The dangers involved with homosexuality rest in the increased likelihood that practicing homosexuality may lead to certain unfortunate consequences, specifically in the areas of health and death.

Virtually all studies on STDs indicate that homosexual activity is more likely to result in the transmission of sexual diseases than heterosexual activity. Sixty-five percent of all AIDS cases in the Unites States since 1981 have been men who engage in homosexual behavior.[7]

An even more staggering statistic is revealed when looking at the impact of homosexuality on suicides. Whatever the causes, the fact remains that homosexuals commit suicide at a higher rate than the rest of the population. We have already mentioned how a large issue dealing with homosexuality is identity confusion. One study revealed that the single largest predictor of mental health was self-acceptance.[8] This sense of personal worth, in addition to a positive take on one's sexual orientation, is necessary for an individuals' mental health. This is especially the case with teenagers, during a time when so many variables are changing and the sense of self is constantly being challenged. Homosexual youth are two to six times more likely to commit suicide than other youths, and 30 percent of all youth suicides are related to sexual identity.[9] Also, 40.3 percent of homosexual youth that were surveyed indicated that they had tried to commit suicide, and another 25.8 percent had given serious thought to it.[10] Because a lot of the issues dealing with homosexuality are psychological, it is easy to understand how the multiplication of these factors can cause intense feelings of anger, loneliness, and despair.

Church Teaching on Homosexuality • • • • • • • •

- **What is the Catholic Church's position on homosexuality?**

The Church makes a distinction between homosexual orientation and homosexual activity. The Church loves those who have a homosexual orientation with all the care and compassion as it does any other person: "[Homosexuals] must be accepted with respect, compassion, and sensitivity. Every sign of unjust discrimination in their regard should be avoided" (*CCC*, 2358).

Regarding homosexual activity, the Church is absolutely opposed to homosexual acts describing the acts as "intrinsically disordered" and "contrary to the natural law" (*CCC*, 2357).

Homosexuals "are called to fulfill God's will in their lives and, if they are Christians, to unite to the sacrifice of the Lord's Cross the difficulties they may encounter from their condition." Furthermore, the *Catechism* teaches, "Homosexual persons are called to chastity. By the virtues of self-mastery that teach them inner freedom, at times by the support of disinterested friendship, by prayer and sacramental grace, they can and should gradually and resolutely approach Christian perfection" (2359).

- **Why is that the position of the Catholic Church?**

The Catholic Church is opposed to sexual activity that is not within the context of marriage and is not open to the possibility of children. The homosexual act is closed to the gift of life and does not take place in the context of a marriage.

- **Can homosexuals get married?**

While there are states that are considering legalizing civil marriages for persons of the same sex, the Catholic Church is opposed to these unions as the Church teaches that marriage is to be between a man and woman.

- **Which Scripture passages are relevant to the issue of homosexuality?**

First, one should remember that scripture passages are not to be taken out of context but always read within the Tradition of the Church.

Romans 1:24–27

1 Corinthians 6:9–10

1 Timothy 1:9–11

HOMOSEXUALITY DILEMMA #1

It is Tami's senior year and she is at the beach on spring break with her best friend, Sonia. They met freshman year and have been inseparable ever since. They are reminiscing about all the memories they have shared and how much fun they had during the past four years. They will attend different colleges next year, but promise that they will remain in close contact. At the end of the conversation, Sonia gets quiet and then makes Tami swear to keep a secret. Tami promises she will, because both of them have shared many secrets in the past. Then Sonia tells her that she is gay and that Tami is the only person she has told. Sonia reassures Tami that she is not attracted to her but needs the support of a friend.

Discussion Questions:

1) How should Tami respond?

2) Should this new information change their friendship?

3) What is your view of homosexual people? Do you know anyone who is homosexual?

4) How are gays and lesbians treated in our society and why?

We have discussed this Tough Choice.

_____

Parent/Guardian Signature

_____

Student Signature

HOMOSEXUALITY DILEMMA #2

Derek and Rick have been friends since kindergarten. During the summer before high school, Derek told Rick that he thinks he is gay. Rick was surprised, but came to accept it as a part of Derek. Derek made him promise to keep his sexual orientation a secret. Both tried out for the basketball team and made it on the junior varsity squad as freshmen. A few weeks later, rumors started flying around the locker room. One particular upperclassman on the team was talking about not wanting a "fairy" being on the team and he looked at Derek. Today, the same person approached Derek and began pushing him around and calling him "fag" and "queer." Other members on the team looked in Derek's direction and laughed or shook their heads, but no one supported him. Derek looks at Rick for help.

Discussion Questions:

1) What should Rick do?

2) Is it Rick's responsibility to say something? Why? What?

3) Even though he made a promise to Derek, should Rick tell a person of authority, like the basketball coach or parents, about the upperclassman's behavior?

4) Is there a chance that Derek may not be gay?

5) Have you ever used derogatory words like "fag" or "queer?" Why?

We have discussed this Tough Choice.

_____

Parent/Guardian Signature

_____

Student Signature

HOMOSEXUALITY DILEMMA #3

Tiffany, a junior in high school, is confused and scared. She knows she is a lesbian but she has not told anyone because she is scared of being rejected by friends and family. Tiffany's family is Catholic, and as a family they attend Mass every Sunday. She has heard her father make "gay" jokes at family parties sometimes. Her mother always introduces Tiffany to her friends' sons as possible dates. Tiffany feels torn between her beliefs and her feelings.

Discussion Questions:

1) What should Tiffany do?

2) How would you react if you were Tiffany's friend?

3) How would you react if you were Tiffany's sister or brother?

4) How should you respond when someone tells a homosexual joke in your presence?

We have discussed this Tough Choice.

_____   _____

Parent/Guardian Signature   Student Signature

Notes

1. Simon Forrest, Grant Biddle, and Stephen Clift. *Talking About Homosexuality in the Secondary School,* Aids Education & Research Trust (AVERT) (1997).

2. Ibid.

3. Gary Remafedi et al. "Demography of Sexual Orientation in Adolescents," *Pediatrics,* 89 (April 1992).

4. New Yorker's Family Research Foundation, Inc., "Statistics on Homosexuality" at http://www.nyfrf.org/homostat.htm

5. Simon Forrest et. al., *Talking About Homosexuality in the Secondary School.*

6. Ibid.

7. Centers for Disease Control, *HIV/AIDS Surveillance Report* 9, no. 2 (May 1998).

8. Scott L. Hershberger and Anthony R. D'Augelli. "The Impact of Victimization on the Mental Health and Suicidality of Lesbian, Gay, and Bisexual Youths" *Developmental Psychology* 31 (1995): 65–74.

9. P. Gibson, "Gay Male and Lesbian Youth Suicide," *Prevention and Intervention in Youth Suicide* ed. M. Feinlab Report to the Secretary's Task Force on Youth Suicide vol. 3. (Washington, D.C.: U.S. Department of Health and Human Services, 1989): 110–142.

10. Curtis D. Proctor and Victor K. Groze, "Risk Factors for Suicide among Gay, Lesbian, and Bisexual Youths" *Social Work* 39 (1994): 504–513.

HONESTY
HONESTY
HONESTY
HONESTY
HONESTY
HONESTY

HONESTY

HONESTY
HONESTY
HONESTY
HONESTY
HONESTY
HONESTY
HONESTY
HONESTY
HONESTY
HONESTY
HONESTY
HONESTY
HONESTY
HONESTY
HONESTY

Overview of Honesty Issues • • • • • • • • • • •

- **What is meant by "honesty dilemmas"?**

  For students, situations involving honesty most often include lying, stealing, cheating, and plagiarism.

- **What is cheating?**

  Cheating is any dishonest behavior meant to bring about one's personal gain, including giving or receiving information in a way that violates rules of conduct.

- **What is plagiarism?**

  Plagiarism is taking ideas or writings from others and passing them off as your own.

- **How common are lying, cheating, and stealing among high school students?**

  A report released in October 2002 by the Josephson Institute of Ethics, *The Ethics of American Youth*, does an excellent job at outlining the occurrence of these honesty dilemmas today. The Josephson Institute also conducted a survey in 1992 and found that the occurrence of lying, cheating, and stealing has increased since ten years ago. The 2002 survey used the responses from 12,000 high-school students. In general, it found that the number of students who cheated on a test increased from 61 percent to 74 percent; the number who stole something within the past year rose from 31 percent to 38 percent; and the number who lied to parents (83 percent to 93 percent) and teachers (69 percent to 83 percent) also increased. These statistics and all of the following information come from this 2002 report.

  Some interesting generalizations were discovered by this study, specifically, the effects of gender, sports participation, religious school attendance, personal religious convictions, and interest in furthering an academic career on issues of honesty.

  Gender was found to be the most significant differentiating factor among high-school students. Females and males cheat and lie at about the same rate, yet girls are less likely to steal or engage in other dishonest practices and have a more positive attitude toward ethics, in general.

  Despite the commonly held notions of teamwork, sacrifice, and character usually associated with participation in sports teams, the study found that such participation does little to build or undermine character. Interestingly, varsity athletes were actually more likely to cheat on exams (78 percent to 73 percent) than nonparticipatory students.

  Another interesting finding was that in the area of honesty, students attending private religious schools do not differ much from their nonreligious school student counterparts. While students attending private religious schools stole less (34 percent to 39 percent), they cheated (78 percent to 72 percent) and lied to parents (95 percent to 91 percent) and to teachers (86 percent to 81 percent) more.

  Students, regardless of school attended, who believed that religion was of great importance to them exhibited similar actions to those who did not value religion so highly. They were less likely to shoplift (34 percent to 38 percent) or lie to get a job (32 percent to 37 percent), and like females, had better attitudes towards the importance of ethics.

  Those in honors or advanced placement classes or who intended to go to college said they lied, cheated, and stole less than those not in the same classes or without college intentions.

  Also, it is reported that while 95 percent of the students agreed with the statement, "It's important to me that people can trust me" and 79 percent agreed that "It's not worth it to lie or cheat because it hurts your character", there was a tremendous increase (9 percent to 43 percent) in the past ten years for students who agreed that "A person has to lie or cheat sometimes in order to succeed."

By themselves, these statistics are revealing and disturbing, but Michael Josephson, president of the Josephson Institute of Ethics, voiced the implicit danger in these findings: "The scary thing is that so many kids are entering the workforce to become corporate executives, politicians, airplane mechanics, and nuclear inspectors with the dispositions and skills of cheaters and thieves."

- **Other than a decline in student values, are there other reasons behind such dishonesty?**

Gary J. Niels, the Upper School Director at Hawken School, in Gates Mills, Ohio, and author of *Academic Practices, School Culture and Cheating Behavior*, explained why students resort to academic dishonesty in the modern world. His findings center on five key areas: social factors, curricular factors, peer influence, teacher clarity and inattention, and school ethos.

Socially, many factors have changed students' perceptions of the world and their role in it. Economic uncertainty has led to a sense of instability. Competition is not as much a desire to excel as it is a struggle to prevent losing.[1] Rather than be excited about the possibilities open to them after they graduate, students worry what the future holds. Niels argues that this fear is demonstrated in the college application process. Currently there is an increase of 50 percent in the number of students applying to college. In the past, students applied to four or five colleges. Those applications per student have increased to ten or more.[2] This highlights the need for students to feel accepted. The fear of alienation causes students to seek out alternative means to succeed.

School curriculum and the educational system are culpable for promoting cheating behavior. The need for teachers to "cover" all the outlined material for their discipline's curriculum leads to a quick, yet shallow survey of dates, people, and events.[3] Covering too much material too quickly requires students to devise ways to integrate such vast amounts of material. According to one study of 6,000 students at thirty-one colleges and universities, business and engineering courses had the highest rates of cheating. Most students reasoned this phenomenon was due to the fact-based nature of the tests.[4] Also, the education system puts a heavy emphasis on the evaluation of student performance through comparison. As Niels states, "Class ranking, national and local percentile rankings on standardized test scores, curve grading, grade point averages, valedictorian and salutatorian are all measures of performance based on competition".[5] Such an atmosphere often generates a "win-at-all-costs" attitude.

Peer influence is another characteristic that influences cheating. In the highly contested teenage battle for claiming and maintaining popularity, problems involving academic dishonesty often develop. When cheating does occur, student witnesses would rather allow the incident to go unreported than risk breaking ranks with their teenage peer group. In addition, the rebelliousness inherent in the act of cheating can cause teenagers to engage in cheating behaviors or be more open to them as a means of gaining social acceptance.

Teachers can also unwittingly help to promote cheating behavior. By failing to explain the relevance and/or purpose of learning a particular topic, teachers encourage cheating.[6] Students need to understand the application of a concept to their lives, or they will view it as a waste of time, will place little value in it, and will look for short cuts. Additionally, the number and frequency of assessment opportunities can play a role.[7] Having only one or two major tests increases the anxiety students feel towards taking those tests, due to the importance of their performing well, and thereby increases the likelihood of academic dishonesty. Also, personality characteristics of teachers affect cheating. Teachers who are viewed as unfriendly or dull, who have low expectations, or who talk down to or display a lack of respect towards students increase the odds that cheating will occur.

Lastly, school ethos can be a determining factor. In her book, *The Good High School*, Sara Lawrence Lightfoot observed that "good schools" display certain core values.[8] These values are embodied by the school and are constantly and consistently reinforced to the student body. When such values are seen as the origin of policies and behavior in the school, they permeate the actions of teachers and students alike. In addition, it is a prime directive that schools convey exactly what an "education" truly is. For students who view assignments, classes, and school careers as a means to an end, it is the responsibility of the school to demonstrate the inherent value that education holds.

- **Hasn't academic dishonesty been something that's been around forever? Why is it a big deal now?**

True, lying, stealing, and cheating all have been around for many years. But one of the earlier answers reveals how this dishonesty problem has increased to record levels. Technology has made certain forms of lying, stealing, and cheating easier to practice. Think about it. It is much easier to lie about not fulfilling obligations using email than it is by using a telephone or telling someone face-to-face. Stealing no longer requires an individual to physically remove an object from a building, only to know a few numbers or be handy with computers. Cheating does not need to occur in the classroom, under the observation of a teacher.

The Internet has opened up the world to many wonderful opportunities, but it has made plagiarism of papers an effortless and time-saving option. A 2002 finding listed over 250 active Internet sites from which students could download term papers.[9] Fortunately, there are also plagiarism detection sites developing, but it underscores the necessity of forming one's own beliefs on honesty. It is easy to be dishonest, but it is imperative that students and adults alike adopt a conviction to be honest.

Church Teaching on Honesty Issues • • • • • •

- **What is the Catholic Church's position on these honesty issues?**
The Catholic Church looks to the eighth commandment on issues of honesty: "You shall not bear false witness against your neighbor." The *Catechism of the Catholic Church* explains: "The eighth commandment forbids misrepresenting the truth in our relations with others. This moral prescription flows from the vocation of the holy people to bear witness to their God who is the truth and wills the truth" (2464).

  In addition, stealing is covered under the seventh commandment: "You shall not steal."

- **Why is that the position of the Catholic Church?**
The Church teaches that God is the source of all truth and that Jesus Christ is Truth. Thus all believers are called to live lives dedicated to truth and justice. This belief is identified in both the Old and New Testaments.

- **What issues are included under the eighth commandment?**
Committing perjury (violating an oath), making rash judgments against another person, pointing out the faults of others when it is not necessary, unjustly harming the reputation of others, encouraging another's immoral behavior, boasting or bragging, and other means by which a person "speaks a falsehood with the intention of deceiving" are among the issues included under the eighth commandment (*CCC*, 2482) .

- **What issues are included under the seventh commandment?**
Stealing encompasses theft and also includes cheating, doing shoddy work on a job, and vandalism.

- **Which Scripture passages are relevant to the issues of honesty?**
Old Testament

  2 Samuel 7:28

  Psalm 119:90

  Proverbs 8:7

  New Testament

  Matthew 5:33–37

  John 1:14

  John 8:44

  John 16:13

  John 18:37

  Acts 24:15–16

  Romans 3:4

  Ephesians 4:24–25

  1 Peter 2:1

  1 John 1:6

HONESTY DILEMMA #1

Ron is attending a pep rally in anticipation for his school's homecoming game. Emotions are high and the atmosphere is electric as the whole school is in a frenzy on a Friday afternoon. Ron is sitting with his best friend, Brandon. They are neighbors and do everything together. However, the two of them are quite different. Brandon often gets into trouble while Ron has a clean record at their school. Brandon has been suspended twice, and according to the school's policy, three suspensions results in automatic expulsion. At one point during the rally, as the cheerleaders lead the crowd in cheers to welcome the team, Brandon starts replacing some of the words of the cheer with inappropriate language. Ron thinks it is funny and laughs. However, Ron then notices a teacher heading in their direction. She has heard the cheer and demands to know who said it. Ron glances around and notices that the two of them are surrounded by members of the opposite sex, so there is no hope in blaming somebody else. The cheer either came from Ron or Brandon. Knowing that using such language during a school function is a suspendable offense, Ron has a choice.

Discussion Questions:

1) Should Ron speak up and take the blame for something his friend did, or should he allow his friend to face the consequences?

2) Would it be different if this was Brandon's first offense?

3) Is it ever okay to lie for a friend? When?

We have discussed this Tough Choice.

_____   _____
Parent/Guardian Signature   Student Signature

HONESTY DILEMMA #2

The Russo children received high marks on their most recent report cards, so their parents decide to take them to dine at their favorite restaurant. The prices are a bit expensive, but the food is well worth it. After a satisfying meal, they decide against having dessert. But when the waitress brings out the dessert samples, the Russos all change their mind and decide to have a dessert item. They finish their dessert and the waitress brings them the bill. The total seems awfully low, and they realize that the waitress accidentally omitted the dessert items from the final bill.

Discussion Questions:

1) Should the family report the missing item on the bill?

2) Would it matter if they had to pay an enormous price for parking?

3) Would it matter if they had never been to the restaurant before and never plan to go there again?

4) What if they knew that if there is an error on the bill, it comes out of the waitress's pay?

5) Does it make a difference if the service was good or bad?

We have discussed this Tough Choice.

_____   _____

Parent/Guardian Signature   Student Signature

HONESTY DILEMMA #3

During September of Derek's senior year, he is working twenty-five hours per week to barely make his insurance payments in addition to paying off the car, gas, and his other expenses. He knows that any accident or speeding ticket would cause his insurance payments to dramatically increase and he knows he couldn't pay for it. In a rush one afternoon Derek pulls out of a store parking lot and doesn't see the small car parked off center behind him. He hits it, obviously damaging its taillights and scratching the bumper. No one saw him. He knows that, if he leaves his name and number, the person will probably call, get his insurance information and file a police report. This will cause his insurance rate to increase and he will have no way to pay the new amount. Derek knows he will end up losing his car if he leaves his number.

Discussion Questions:

1) What should Derek do?

2) Does it matter how much damage was done?

3) Does it matter that Derek knows no one saw him?

4) How would you feel if you were the person whose car was hit and Derek did not leave his name and address?

We have discussed this Tough Choice.

_____

Parent/Guardian Signature

_____

Student Signature

HONESTY DILEMMA #4

Kent, Phil, and Brian decide to go on a trip to the city, about three hours from where they live. After about two hours on the road the group needs to stop and get gas. Kent pulls up to a gas station and goes inside to use the restroom. While Kent is in the restroom, Phil and Brian fill the car up with gas. Kent comes out of the gas station and the three friends head off down the road towards Chicago. About forty-five minutes from the gas station the three friends realize that no one paid for the gas. Kent thought that Phil and Brian had paid for the gas while he was in the bathroom, and Phil and Brian thought that Kent had paid for the gas when he was in the gas station.

Discussion Questions:

1) Should the guys turn around and pay for the gas?

2) Should they pay for the gas on the way back home from their trip?

3) Should they not worry about paying the gas station back since they committed an honest mistake?

We have discussed this Tough Choice.

_____   _____

Parent/Guardian Signature   Student Signature

HONESTY DILEMMA #5

Gina is a high-school student who has been working at a small convenience store for the past six months. There are only five employees in addition to the owner, so she gets to know everyone well. The store does not make a lot of money, but the owner loves what she does because she gets to constantly interact with people. One week, Gina receives her paycheck. She puts it away and finishes her shift. When she gets home she takes it out, looks at it, and realizes there is a mistake. A decimal point has been moved, so instead of receiving $23.50, the paycheck is written for $235.00. Gina knows that the owner does not keep close records, so it would be unlikely for the owner to check on the mistake, but she also knows that the difference in money would come out of the store's profits.

Discussion Questions:

1) What should Gina do?

2) What if the owner could easily check the mistake? How would that make a difference?

3) Does the amount of money make a difference? For example, what if it was five dollars added to the paycheck?

4) What if it was a large company where Gina didn't know the owner so well and the profits were great? How would that matter?

We have discussed this Tough Choice.

_____

Parent/Guardian Signature

_____

Student Signature

CHEATING & PLAGIARISM DILEMMA #1

Paul and Michael are long-time friends. They both attend a school that enforces a strict honor code. The honor code policy states that students may not receive help from or assist in giving help to another student on a paper or test. Further, any student who notices the sharing of such help is obligated to report this violation to a school official. If that student does not, they are just as guilty of the infraction as the person who either gave or received help.

Both Paul and Michael are taking a trigonometry class. This has been Paul's most difficult subject all year and he has been preparing for weeks for the midterm exam. He enters the testing room and sits behind Michael's girlfriend Suzie. The teacher comes into the room and passes out the exam. After a few minutes of taking the test, Paul sits back in his chair and stretches.

As he leans back he notices that Suzie is cheating off of the test next to her. When the test is over the teacher collects the exams. Paul believes that he is the only one who noticed Suzie cheating.

Discussion Questions:

1) Should Paul report the dishonesty to the teacher? Does it matter if Suzie had never been caught cheating before?

2) If you were Paul's friend and he told you this story over lunch what would you advise him to do?

3) If the school does not have an honor code, does his responsibility change?

4) How do Suzie's actions affect Paul personally?

5) Would Paul's responsibility be different if the teacher was not in the room for the test?

We have discussed this Tough Choice.

_____   _____
Parent/Guardian Signature   Student Signature

CHEATING & PLAGIARISM DILEMMA #2

Lincoln High School has a no defined cheating policy. Mr. Evans assigned a lengthy worksheet on the Constitution on Monday. It is due Wednesday. Brant finished the assignment late Tuesday night and came to school Wednesday morning. Maurice, a good friend of Brant, hurriedly came to Brant and asked to copy his homework. Maurice said he didn't have time to do the work because of other homework and his after school job.

Discussion Questions:

1) What should Brant do?

2) If Maurice will fail the class by not turning in the homework, does that change how Brant handles the situation?

3) What if Brant and Maurice were not good friends but just acquaintances?

4) Why is cheating wrong? Who are the people cheating effects in this example?

We have discussed this Tough Choice.

_____

Parent/Guardian Signature

_____

Student Signature

CHEATING & PLAGIARISM DILEMMA #3

Kristin and Bernice are not close friends but they have known each other throughout high school and get along well enough. They discover that they want to go to the same out-of-state college. Their senior years they take AP English together and one of their assignments is to put together a fine arts magazine with poems, short stories, and essays by the students. Bernice is the editor. Kristin turns in some very well written poems that won her some local awards. Her poems are about to be published in the high school magazine. Bernice discovers that Kristin copied the poems from the college's fine arts magazine. The writers are college students who are not famous. It would be difficult for anyone around the high school to know that Kristin has plagiarized someone else's work.

Discussion Questions:

1) What should Bernice do?

2) Would it matter if Bernice and Kristin were good friends? What if they disliked each other?

3) How does this situation effect the local awards Kristin has already won?

4) What if Kristin changed approximately ten words in a hundred-line poem? Is this as severe?

5) How are taking someone's ideas and taking someone's possessions different? Are they different?

We have discussed this Tough Choice.

_____

Parent/Guardian Signature

_____

Student Signature

CHEATING & PLAGIARISM DILEMMA #4

Sharon spent most of last night at her best friend Laura's house, helping her to get over a breakup.

She knew she had a difficult literature test she had to take the next day. The test makes up one-third of the course grade.

Sharon did not have a chance to study and now she might not do well on the test. Lisa, who was a mutual friend of Sharon and Laura, heard of Sharon's plight. Lisa had taken the same test earlier in the day. Before Sharon's class met, Lisa approached Sharon in the hall, slipped her a piece of paper with a smile, and walked away in silence. When Sharon opened the paper, she saw all the answers to the test. It was very small, so Sharon could easily hold it in her palm while she took the test. She knew that cheating was wrong, but it wasn't her fault that she couldn't study last night. She was just being a good friend.

Discussion Questions:

1) Is Sharon justified in cheating on the test?

2) What if it were a lesser quiz rather than an important test?

3) Why do people cheat? What purpose does it serve?

4) Are there situations where cheating is acceptable?

We have discussed this Tough Choice.

_____

Parent/Guardian Signature

_____

Student Signature

CHEATING & PLAGIARISM DILEMMA #5

Sandra is a cheerleader and vice president of the student council. Due to the upcoming homecoming game and freshman class elections, this week has been exhausting for her. She has been overburdened by her many responsibilities. Last week, Sandra's biology teacher assigned a research project. The night before it is due, while talking on the phone, a classmate mentions his difficulty with the project. Only then does Sandra remember the assignment. She begins to panic because all of the libraries are closed. However, she remembers that the teacher recommended that she use the Internet as a resource. While Sandra is searching the web, she comes across an essay written by a college student on the exact topic that had been assigned. Sandra is fairly sure that she can simply copy this paper into a word processor and turn it in as her own work without getting caught. However, she knows that if she does get caught, she could risk flunking biology.

Discussion Questions:

1) What should Sandra do?

2) Would it matter if the assignment was not due the next day ?

3) Would copying only a few paragraphs or sentences still be considered cheating? How many?

4) Would simply rearranging the words from the Internet site into her own words, without citing the Internet as a source for her research, be considered cheating?

5) Outside of getting caught, what other deterrents face Sandra?

We have discussed this Tough Choices.

_____   _____

Parent/Guardian   Signature Student Signature

CHEATING & PLAGIARISM DILEMMA #6

Brandi is currently in a class that she really enjoys. She respects the teacher, Mr. Schultz, but the class is difficult. Brandi is not doing well in the class. She has an "F" average and needs to get at least a "C" on the final exam in order to pass the class. She has studied very hard for the exam. However, while taking the exam Brandi quickly realizes she is not doing well. She just cannot remember some of the material. She starts to look anxiously at the clock. Suddenly, another teacher comes into the room and informs Mr. Schultz that there is an emergency phone call for him. Mr. Schultz tells the class, "I have to leave for a few minutes. You are on your honor." Then he leaves. About thirty seconds after he leaves, Brandi hears some of her fellow classmates whispering. She looks around and sees some students with their books and notebooks out, looking up answers. Others are sharing their answers. It would be easy for Brandi to cheat on this exam as well.

Discussion Questions:

1) What should Brandi do?

2) What if this test determined whether or not she graduated from high school?

3) Should Brandi inform Mr. Schultz about her classmates' dishonesty?

4) Is it ever okay to cheat?

5) What constitutes "cheating"?

We have discussed this Tough Choice.

_____   _____

Parent/Guardian Signature   Student Signature

CHEATING & PLAGIARISM DILEMMA #7

Calculators today can do a lot more than just add or subtract. Technology is so sophisticated today that calculators can perform calculus problems and run short programs. Some students have used this to their advantage on tests by programming formulas and sample problems into the calculators. Brad just got a brand new sophisticated graphic calculator, and is learning how to use its many buttons. It is Friday and Brad has a difficult test on Monday in algebra. He has been struggling with the material and is really worried about the test. Brad confides with his classmate Clark that he feels stressed out. Clark tells him that he is not concerned because he programmed all the formulas into his calculator. He shows Brad how to do it and justifies that it is not cheating because in the real world one can always look up formulas in a book. Brad agrees, but remembers that his teacher specifically told the class that it is important to memorize all the formulas and to understand how to use them. Brad knows that his math teacher never checks the programs on calculators before a test, so he probably would not get caught.

Discussion Questions:

1) Should Brad program the formulas into the calculator?

2) Is this cheating? Why or why not?

3) Should Brad report Clark for programming the formulas in his calculator?

4) If Brad does not get caught, does that make his action okay?

5) If everyone else is doing it, does that make his action less wrong?

6) How would your parents feel if they knew you cheated? How would a younger sibling feel if they knew you cheated?

We have discussed this Tough Choice.

_____   _____
Parent/Guardian Signature   Student Signature

CHEATING & PLAGIARISM DILEMMA #8

James was daydreaming in class, when he was called to attention by the teacher's movement around the room. James asked a classmate what the teacher was doing and was told that he was checking to see if the students had gotten their progress reports signed by their parents. School policy required all progress reports to be signed and returned to school the following day. That James had forgotten to do this was not completely true. Due to some personal problems, James had had a poor semester in the classroom. He had three D's and four F's. That kind of report card certainly would get him grounded and prevent him from going to the upcoming dance. Therefore, he had neglected to show the report to his parents. At James' school, any student who does not return a signed progress report receives a call home from each teacher. James knows what his mother's signature looks like and is fairly certain he could forge it on the progress report.

Discussion Questions:

1) What should James do?

2) If you were James' parent and found out about this situation, what would you tell James?

3) Is it ever permissible to lie or cheat?

4) Does cheating on something small really matter?

We have discussed this Tough Choice.

_____

Parent/Guardian Signature

_____

Student Signature

STEALING DILEMMA #1

Terry has been an employee at a fast food restaurant for the past six months. He expects to receive a raise shortly. Last week, he saw one of his coworkers sell a meal to a customer and pocket the money (about $5). The coworker knows Terry saw him do it, but Terry feels awkward confronting him because he's Terry's friend and Terry doesn't want to risk that friendship. Terry knows he could get fired or lose his promotion if the manager finds out that he knew about the theft.

Discussion Questions:

1) What should Terry do?

2) To whom does Terry owe more allegiance in this situation?

3) If you do not think Terry should tell the owner, would your opinion change if more than $5 was pocketed?

4) What if Terry did not like the coworker?

5) What is Terry's responsibility to the business?

6) Would it matter if the coworker handed the $5 to a homeless man who was seated outside the restaurant?

We have discussed this Tough Choice.

_____   _____
Parent/Guardian Signature   Student Signature

STEALING DILEMMA #2

Ted and John have been friends for five years. One afternoon they go to the mall together to get some new clothes for school. While at a popular clothing store, John sees Ted take a pair of shorts off the rack and put it under his shirt. Ted doesn't know that John saw him take the shorts. The stores shoplifting policy is prominently displayed stating that security will be called and violators will be prosecuted to the "fullest extent of the law". Ted motions to John that he'd like to leave the store and continue shopping elsewhere.

Discussion Questions:

1) What should John do?

2) Should you risk a friend being mad at you if it means keeping him or her out of trouble like this?

3) If the store manager saw Ted stealing, what should John do?

4) What do you think would happen if John was accused of helping Ted steal?

5) If John doesn't tell the owner, is he just as guilty as Ted in stealing the shorts?

We have discussed this Tough Choice.

_____

Parent/Guardian Signature

_____

Student Signature

STEALING DILEMMA #3

The school gym is located in an area separate from the rest of the school. Students are not admitted into the facility unless they are in gym class and accompanied by the gym teacher who has the key. Benny has just completed gym class when one of his fellow classmates discovers that the cash he had in his gym bag is missing. This student tells the teacher. The teacher keeps everyone after the bell and summons the principal when nobody confesses. After a lecture, the principal says that he will call each of the students individually into his office. If nobody confesses or if the names of the thieves are not provided, the entire class will be suspended until the stolen cash is returned. All tests, quizzes, homework, and assignments missed during suspension are given automatic "zeroes". However, ratting on a fellow classmate is seen as an unpopular move. Benny did not steal the property, but knows who did.

Discussion Questions:

1) What should Benny do?

2) Would your answer change if you were the student whose money was stolen?

3) Is it ever okay to withhold the truth when someone directly asks for it?

We have discussed this Tough Choice.

_____   _____

Parent/Guardian Signature   Student Signature

Notes

1. Christopher Lasch, *The Minimal Self: Psychic Survival in Troubled Times* (New York: Norton, 1984), 72.

2. "Record Number of Applicants Are Reported by the Top Colleges," *New York Times*, 18 February 1996.

3. Grant Wiggins, "The Futility of Trying to Teach Everything of Importance" *Educational Leadership* (Alexandria, VA: ASCD, November 1989): 44–59.

4. Reported by Donald McCabe during a "National Teleconference Addressing Issues of Academic Dishonesty" from Bowling Green State University (29 September 1995).

5. Gary J. Niels, "Academic Practices, School Culture and Cheating Behavior" at http://www.hawken.edu/odris/cheating/cheating.html

6. Ellis Evans and Delores Craig, "Teacher and Student Perceptions of Academic Cheating in Middle and Senior High Schools," *Journal of Educational* Research, 84, no.1, (September/October 1990), 49.

7. Ibid.

8. Sara L. Lightfoot, *The Good High School: Portraits of Character and Culture*, New York: Basic Books, 1983.

9. Presentation by Margaret Fain and Peggy Bates, "Cheating 101: Paper Mills and You", given as part of the Teaching Effectiveness Seminars held at Coastal Carolina University, 5 March 1999. Revised March 26, 2001, and found at http://www.coastal.edu/library/papermil.htm

SEXUALITY
SEXUALITY
SEXUALITY
SEXUALITY
SEXUALITY
SEXUALITY

SEXUALITY

SEXUALITY
SEXUALITY
SEXUALITY
SEXUALITY
SEXUALITY
SEXUALITY
SEXUALITY
SEXUALITY
SEXUALITY
SEXUALITY
SEXUALITY
SEXUALITY
SEXUALITY
SEXUALITY
SEXUALITY
SEXUALITY

Overview of Sexuality Issues • • • • • • • • •

- ## What is sex?
It is very hard to define sex in a way that all people agree upon. Most often, the term *sex* refers to vaginal sexual intercourse. However, various components of sexual activity, such as oral sex, masturbation, and other forms of genital stimulation, all should be considered when discussing the topic of sex. For this discussion, the term sex refers to heterosexual vaginal intercourse.

- ## How many teenagers are sexually active?
According to one 1997 study of teens, 48 percent of females and 49 percent of males admitted to participating in sexual intercourse at least once.[1] However, a 1998 survey revealed that two out of every three males and females had engaged in sex by the age of 18.[2] The exact numbers are difficult to determine because teens may admit to sexual activity solely for peer acceptance. The fact remains that many teens are sexually active.

- ## Why is having sex such a major decision?
The decision to participate in sexual intercourse has lifelong implications. The biggest mistake people make is thinking that sex is over when the intercourse ends. Every time someone chooses to engage in sexual activity, there are emotional, psychological, social, physical, and spiritual consequences that result from the experience, no matter how wanted and enjoyable the experience may be.

- ## What are these emotional and psychological consequences of having sex?
Emotionally and psychologically, placing oneself in a vulnerable position creates a complex residual effect influenced by the motivations or reasons for engaging in the sexual activity, the persons involved, the relationship of the individuals before and after the act, the physical side effects, and the number and type of people who are made aware of the experience, just to name a few. One's attitudes, which depend on emotions and other consequences, can range from satisfaction to personal hatred and loathing. Feelings of power, virility, conquest, and popularity are just as likely as feelings of self-doubt, inadequacy, guilt, and shame. Neither of these extremes is beneficial to those individuals participating in sexual intercourse because they focus only on the self. Because many people who are sexually active engage in intercourse for selfish reasons, the dichotomy of feelings will continue to persist. Any sexual activity that is not meant to reveal true love of the other person, regardless of individual needs or desires, carries selfish emotional and psychological baggage.

- ## What are the social consequences of having sex?
A social consequence of having sex involves how the act affects an individual's relationship with his or her partner, peers, parents, and others. Sexual activity does not take place in a vacuum. When adolescents or adults engage in sexual activity, very rarely is it kept as a secret between the two individuals involved. Word of the experience is typically made known to friends, unknown peers, adults, and even parents. One thing individuals who engage in sexual activity cannot control is the reactions and opinions of individuals who learn of their experience. In each case, the one-time experience of sexual intimacy affects how each individual is viewed.

Another social consequence is the creation of a culture that is desensitized to sex. The more casual sex is practiced and/or accepted by people, the more it becomes the norm for the culture in which they live. Sex can be transformed from the ultimate expression of committed love into an object that is free to be given to anyone at anytime. When sexual intercourse loses value, a person loses respect. In and of itself, this is a problem. It is also a problem for society because it allows casual attitudes and behaviors to develop regarding human sexuality. Two of the biggest results of this desensitization are sexual harassment and rape. These issues are committed by individuals towards others but have their roots in the devaluing of sexual intimacy.

- **What is sexual harassment? How common is sexual harassment among teenagers?**

Sexual harassment is any unwanted or unwelcome behavior, comments, touching, or joking of a sexual nature that makes an individual awkward or uncomfortable, or that creates a hostile environment. Once experienced, it should be made aware to the perpetrating individual that such acts, words, gestures, or suggestions are inappropriate. In addition, an authority figure should be informed of the problem.

Much like its occurrence in the rest of society, sexual harassment among teenagers has only recently been given the attention it deserves. Therefore, there is not much information that reflects how often it occurs. A 1993 study found that four out of every five students in grades 8 through 11 had experienced some form of sexual harassment in their school life, including 85 percent of girls and 75 percent of boys.[3] The National School Safety Center News Service admitted that the most "overlooked and underreported offense today" was sexual harassment.[4] This is a problem that needs to be discussed and whose cause needs to be understood.

- **How common is rape among teenagers?**

Rape occurs in very similar numbers among teenagers as it does among the rest of society. It is extremely difficult to grasp the true number of rapes due to the fact that so few are reported. Some statistics regarding teenage rape include:[5]

> nearly all female teenage victims know their attacker
> the risk of rape is four times higher for women aged sixteen to twenty-four than for any other age group
> 38 percent of all women who have been raped were fourteen- to seventeen-years old at the time of the attack
> 56 percent of teenage girls who are raped are date-raped
> 30 percent of teenage girls who are raped are raped by a friend
> 11 percent of teenage girls who are raped are raped by a boyfriend
> 78 percent of teenage victims do not tell their parents about the incident
> 71 percent of teenage victims tell a friend that they were raped
> Six percent of teenage victims report the assault to the police
> 75 percent of acquaintance rapes involve alcohol

It is important to see that while very few rapes are reported to police or to parents, individuals who are raped usually tell a friend or a peer. This highlights the importance of the role that friends can play in helping victims to take the right steps to deal with the aftereffects of the crime.

- **What should be done for a friend who has been raped?**

According to Call Rape, Inc. there are a number of important steps that can be taken to help the victim physically, emotionally, and psychologically:[6]

> Believe and empower the victim.
> Recognize the victim's strengths and survival skills.
> Speak to the victim as an equal.
> Make sure all emergency needs are met.
> Ask about how the victim is feeling and let the person know that it is normal to feel angry, fearful, or guilty.
> Allow the victim to talk, if he or she chooses to do so.
> Assure the victim that he or she is not to blame, it is the fault of the criminal.
> Allow the victim to gain control over the situation. Ask permission to do anything. These types of questions allow the victim to make decisions that help him or her regain control.

Identify the most immediate problem facing the victim and help him or her discover ways to solve the problem.

Let the victim know what he or she can anticipate will happen, including visits to the hospital, the criminal justice system, etc.

There are also some things that a friend *should avoid doing*. One should *never*:

insinuate that the victim could be blamed or ask questions that cause the victim to feel this way

tell the victim that everything is all right or that you know how he or she feels (Everything *is not* all right, and you *do not* know how he or she feels.)

touch the victim unless he or she specifically asks you to do so

judge the victim's conduct, force the victim to discuss the details, or impose your opinions on the situation.

There are few important things that need to be done for the victim.[7] Once he or she is in a safe place, away from the attacker, a friend should take the victim to a hospital emergency room. For the sake of evidence, it is important that, if possible, the victim does not shower or change clothes. Once the victim is at the emergency room, the police can be called. The doctor in the emergency room will give the victim a physical exam, check for injuries, and collect evidence. A victim will then be given a blood test to check for pregnancy and diseases. The risk of getting a sexually transmitted disease during a rape is five to ten percent. The doctor can then inform the victim of what options are available to him or her, including filing police reports, scheduling follow-up visits, and explaining the availability of counseling services. Refer to support services offered by the Catholic social service agencies in your diocese.

- **What are the physical consequences of having sex?**

Physically, the greatest consequences of sexual activity are pregnancy and sexually transmitted diseases. The risk of these two potential outcomes is higher for teenagers than the rest of society.

In terms of pregnancy, nearly one million teenage women become pregnant every year.[8] This number represents 10 percent of all women aged fifteen to nineteen and 19 percent of all teenage women who have had sexual intercourse. Seventy-eight percent of these pregnancies were unintended.[9] There are other problems for pregnant teens besides having to care for their children. Of all the teens who become pregnant, only one-third graduate from high school.[10] In addition, children born to teenage women have lower birth weights than those born to older women.[11] These children are more likely to perform poorly in school[12] and are at a greater risk of abuse and neglect.[13]

As for sexually transmitted diseases, or STDs, the numbers also paint a bleak picture for teenagers. Each year, three million teens acquire an STD.[14] The most common STDs are: genital herpes, gonorrhea, human papilloma virus (HPV), chlamydia, syphilis, pubic lice, hepatitis B, and human immunodeficiency virus (HIV). More information on these STDs follows:

Genital Herpes
Genital herpes is an STD caused by the herpes simplex virus (HSV). HSV-type 1 commonly causes fever blisters on the mouth or face, while HSV-type 2 affects the genital area. HSV-1 and HSV-2 are transmitted through direct contact, including kissing, sexual contact, or skin-to-skin contact. Most cases of genital herpes involve no symptoms outside of periodic blisters or lesions. There is no cure for genital herpes. Once infected, people remain infected for life.[15]

Gonorrhea
Gonorrhea is a disease caused by bacteria called *Neiserria gonorrhea* found in the mucus areas of the body, semen, or vaginal fluids and transmitted by sexual contact. Males with

gonorrhea may experience painful urination, and both sexes may experience a pus-like discharge. Gonorrhea can lead to pelvic inflammatory disease (PID) or urinary tract problems and it can spread to other parts of the body, if left untreated. This disease can be treated with antibiotics, however damage already done cannot be reversed. Teens have higher rates of gonorrhea than do sexually active men and women aged twenty to forty-four.[16] In a single act of unprotected sex with an infected partner, a teenage woman has a 50 percent chance of contracting gonorrhea.[17]

Human Papilloma Virus (HPV)—Genital Warts

HPV is the most common STD in the United States, affecting anywhere from ten to twenty-four million people, including one-third of all women.[18] It can have no visible signs or may involve painful genital warts. Although the warts can be removed, there is no known cure for HPV. HPV causes more than 90 percent of all cervical cancer, which kills 4,500 women each year.[19]

Chlamydia

Chlamydia, caused by the bacterium *Chlamydia trachomatis*, is the most common bacterial STD in this country. Most people infected with chlamydia are unaware of it because it usually shows no symptoms. When diagnosed, it can be treated with antibiotics. If left untreated, it can cause infertility, pelvic pain, damage to women's fallopian tubes, and PID. Chlamydia is more common among teenagers than among adults. Between 10 and 29 percent of sexually active teenage women and 10 percent of sexually active teenage men tested for STDs are found to have chlamydia.[20]

Syphilis

Syphilis is an STD caused by the bacterium *Treponema pallidum* and is passed from person to person through direct contact with a syphilis sore, often called a chancre. While it is spread through sexual contact, it cannot be spread by toilet seats, door knobs, hot tubs, swimming pools, or sharing of clothing. Though treatable with antibiotics, left untreated it can lead to enlarged lymph nodes, hepatitis, kidney disease, meningitis, diseases of the heart valves, miscarriages, and insanity. Much like chlamydia and gonorrhea, teens and young adults have the highest rates of syphilis in America.[21]

Pubic Lice (Crabs)

Pubic lice are very small creatures that live in the pubic hair and cause discomfort and itching. They are transmitted through sexual contact and feed off the infected person's skin. Crabs can also be spread by sheets, towels, or shared clothing. Pubic lice lay eggs at the bottom of pubic hair shafts. Pubic lice are treated with a shampoo or lotion.

Hepatitis B

Hepatitis B is the most common STD in the world, with 300,000 new cases annually. Symptoms include a yellowing of the skin, tiredness, dark urine, and gray colored stool. Hepatitis B can cause severe liver damage, resulting in cancer or cirrhosis of the liver. Forty to fifty percent of children born to mothers infected with hepatitis B develop liver cancer.[22]

Human Immunodeficiency Virus (HIV)

HIV impairs cells of the immune system, destroying the body's ability to fight off certain infections. HIV is not the same as acquired immune deficiency syndrome (AIDS), but it can, and usually does, lead to AIDS. There are virtually no signs that an individual has HIV during the first few years he or she is infected. But as the immune system deteriorates, a variety of complications surface, including swollen glands, weight loss, and skin lesions. While recent years have seen drugs that slow the progression of HIV, there are no known cures. People with AIDS usually die from the complications brought along by other ailments. In 1997, HIV infection was the seventh leading cause of death among people aged fifteen to twenty-four.[23]

- **Are there birth control methods that protect against pregnancy and sexually transmitted diseases?**

Of course, birth control methods, or contraceptives, do exist. However, the myth that they protect against pregnancy and STDs is just that, a myth. Here is some information on the most popular contraceptives:[24]

Norplant

Norplant involves inserting six small capsules under the skin of the woman's upper arm. These capsules constantly release small amounts of the hormone, progestin, which prevents the release of an egg and thickens the cervical mucus to keep the sperm from joining the egg. It is 99.5 percent effective in preventing pregnancy, but is not effective in preventing the spread of sexually transmitted diseases. Norplant protects against pregnancy for five years, but the possible side effects include irregular bleeding, headaches, nausea, depression, nervousness, dizziness, and weight gain or loss.

Depo-Provera

Depo-Provera acts much the same way Norplant does, only it is injected into the muscle and lasts for twelve weeks.

Birth Control Pill

The "pill" is taken once a day and has the same effects that Norplant and Depo-Provera do. It is 95 to 99 percent effective in preventing pregnancy, but not effective in preventing sexually transmitted infections. The pill can cause some of the same side effects as Norplant and Depo-Provera, but also may cause blood clots, heart attacks, and strokes in some extreme cases.

Condom

Condoms are thin pieces of latex, plastic, or animal tissue placed over the penis to prevent the sperm from joining the egg. Condoms are only 86 to 97 percent effective for both pregnancy and STD prevention, due to the fact that some of them break or are misapplied during intercourse.

Diaphragm/Cervical Cap/Female Condom/Contraceptive Foam

This method involves placing a latex cup (diaphragm), latex cap (cervical cap), latex female condom, or contraceptive foam in the vagina to prevent the sperm from joining the egg. The diaphragm is 80 to 94 percent effective at preventing pregnancy. The cervical cap is 80 to 91 percent for women who have never had a child and 60 to 74 percent for women who have given birth. Contraceptive foam is 74 to 95 percent effective in preventing pregnancy. The female condom prevents pregnancy 79 to 95 percent of the time. Of these four, only the female condom offers any protection against sexually transmitted diseases, and even then, it is not a sure thing.

Sterilization

Tubal ligation/sterilization permanently severs the woman's tubes through which the sperm joins the egg, and vasectomies permanently sever a man's vas deferens that carry sperm. These surgical procedures are 99.5 to 99.9 percent effective at preventing pregnancy, but not effective against STDs.

IUD (Intrauterine Device)

An IUD involves placing a small plastic device into the uterus. The IUD contains copper or hormones that may prevent the sperm from joining the egg. The shape of the device may prevent a fertilized egg from implanting in the wall of the uterus. IUDs are 98 to 99.4 percent effective at preventing pregnancy but not effective against sexually transmitted diseases. IUDs have been known to lead to pelvic inflammatory disease and in teenagers can cause increased menstrual bleeding and uterine cramping.

Withdrawal

Withdrawal involves a man removing his penis from the vagina before he ejaculates, preventing the sperm from joining the egg. This is 81 to 96 percent effective in preventing pregnancy but not effective in preventing the spread of STDs.

Natural Family Planning

Natural Family Planning involves a couple charting a woman's menstrual cycle and measuring her body temperature. Couples abstain from intercourse during days in which the woman is fertile. This method is 75 to 99 percent effective at preventing pregnancy but not effective at preventing sexually transmitted diseases. However, if this is practiced in a committed marriage, there are no worries of sexually transmitted diseases, unless one or both of the partners has engaged in sexual intercourse prior to marriage. This is the only form of family planning approved by the Church.

- **Have most sexually active teens made free choices to be so?**

  Actually, a lot of times, teens do not intend to engage in sexual intercourse. Many times they are pressured into it either by their partner, peer group, or society. Three out of every four girls and over half of all boys report that girls who have sex do so because their boyfriends want them to.[25] Ninety-three percent of teenage women indicated that their first experience of sexual intercourse was voluntary, but one-quarter of these women said it was unwanted.[26] The younger women are when they first have intercourse, the more likely it is that the sex is unwanted or not done voluntarily. For example, seven out of ten girls who had sex before the age of thirteen felt this way.[27]

- **How do sexually active teens feel about their sexual experiences?**

  A majority of both teenage boys and girls who are sexually active wish they had waited. Nearly 80 percent of teenage females and nearly 60 percent of teenage males stated that they wish they had waited until they were older to have sex.[28]

- **How does the issue of sex relate to other issues teens face (e.g., alcohol, drugs)?**

  Teenagers who engage in such risky behaviors are more likely to have sexual intercourse. One 1995 study revealed that students were two to three times more likely to be sexually active if they drank, smoked cigarettes, or used marijuana.[29] The opposite effect is also true. Adolescent males aged twelve to sixteen who had engaged in sexual intercourse were four times more likely to smoke cigarettes and six times more likely to have used alcohol than boys from the same age group who reported that they were virgins. Likewise, adolescent females who had had sex were seven times more likely to smoke and ten times more likely to use marijuana than adolescent females who were virgins.[30]

- **Is there anything that can be done to influence or help teenagers make the decision to delay having sexual intercourse?**

  Yes, there is. Interestingly, teens say that their families have the biggest influence on whether or not they become sexually active. Parental supervision and feelings of warmth, love, and caring from parents delay the onset of adolescent sexual intercourse.[31] According to Advocates for Youth, adolescents who discuss topics of sexuality with their parents are more likely to delay becoming sexually active. Roughly

70 percent of teenagers admitted that they were ready to listen to things parents believe they were not ready to hear.[32] The same percentage of teens reported that a lack of communication between a girl and her parents is often the reason teenage girls become pregnant.[33]

There is also evidence that the more active teenagers are in other areas of life, the less sexually active they are. In the high school, this can take the form of extra-curricular activities, academics, or spiritual life. One survey found that female athletes, playing one or more sports, are more likely to remain abstinent and delay their first act of sexual intercourse.[34] Compared to the previously mentioned average of nearly half of all adolescents being sexually active, the number of sexually active students who are identified as high achieving juniors or seniors was only 26 percent.[35] Lastly, teenagers who stated that religion and prayer were important to them waited until later to have their first sexual experience than other teens.[36]

What does this mean? It points to the fact that parents play a tremendous role in the decisions their children make. This role carries with it a great responsibility. Parents must talk to their children and set expectations for their children. Also, it reveals that perhaps teenagers engage in sex because they have nothing better to do. A possible solution for families, schools, and communities would be to create more opportunities and activities in which teenagers could participate and by which parents could encourage and support their child's participation. Such involvement would reveal the value parents place in their children's actions and decisions and create an environment in which students could freely discuss issues with their families.

Church Teaching on Sexuality • • • • • • • • • •

- **What is the Catholic Church's position on sexual issues?**

If one had to write one sentence to summarize Catholic Church teachings on sexual matters it would be this: All sexual activity must be both unitive (in the context of marriage) and procreative (open to the possibility of children). All sexual activity outside of marriage and that is not open to children is morally forbidden. The *Catechism* states that sex "is not something simply biological, but concerns the innermost being of the human person as such" (2361).

Each person is called to the virtue of chastity—"the successful integration of sexuality within the person and thus the inner unity of man in his bodily and spiritual being" (2337). Chastity insists that we are able to control our passions. This is accomplished through prayer, obedience to God's commandments, self-knowledge, and the ability to handle oneself when situations arise which tempt one's chastity.

The Church also speaks out against the practices of lust (desire for self-serving sexual desire), masturbation (the deliberate stimulation of the genital organs in order to derive sexual pleasure), fornication (sex between unmarried persons), pornography (real or simulated sexual acts in order to display them to a third party), prostitution (the exchange of sexual acts for payment), and rape (forcing sexual intimacy on another person).

- **Why is that the position of the Catholic Church?**

The Church holds that God created men and women in his likeness. God orders our activity "toward the goods of marriage and the flourishing of family life"(2333). Our society's future depends greatly on the way we live out our relationships between men and women.

As the basis for the position, the *Catechism* states: "*Sexuality* affects all aspects of the human person in the unity of his body and soul. It especially concerns affectivity, the capacity to love and to procreate, and in a more general way the aptitude for forming bonds of communion with others" (2332). Thus, our sexuality is a major part of who we are as individuals and as a human race.

- **Are married people called to be chaste too?**

All the baptized are called to chastity. Single people are called to live a chaste life by abstaining from all sexual activity. Priests, religious sisters and brothers, and others who consecrate themselves to celibacy give themselves in a special way to God in service of others. Married people are called to live "conjugal chastity" meaning they are committed solely to one another.

- **What is the Church's position on contraception?**

The Catholic Church is opposed to the use of contraception. This includes all methods explained on pages 136–137 that are unnatural ways of regulating childbirth. Remember, God demands that every sexual act be within marriage and open to procreation. Contraception unnaturally attempts to close off this possibility.

- **Which Scripture passages are relevant to the issue of sexuality discussed in this section?**

Old Testament

Genesis 1:27–28

Genesis 2:24

Jeremiah 13:27

New Testament

Matthew 5:27–28

Matthew 19:4–6

1 Corinthians 6:9–10

1 Corinthians 6:15–20

Galatians 5:22–24

1 John 3:3

SEXUALITY DILEMMA #1

Maggie always used to enjoy mathematics, but this year has been a little different. The teacher, Mr. Johnson, is a very difficult teacher. He knows mathematics extremely well; however, he seems to treat female students unfairly. Maggie herself has felt this treatment. She remembers numerous occasions when Mr. Johnson ignored her questions in class because he didn't feel they were worth answering. Also, she felt that he had graded her and other female students' tests more harshly than the male students. When some of the female students approached him about it, he just said that they were being overly sensitive and that they should grow up. Maggie felt that the girls' concerns were justified, and she realized that she wouldn't mind having a different math teacher.

The situation took an ugly turn last week. One of the female students went to administration and complained that Mr. Johnson had sexually harassed her and other female students. Then other girls came forward and supported her story. Mr. Johnson was under investigation for harassment and, until the matter was sorted out, he had to leave the school. A couple of days after the accusation, Maggie overheard some of the girls talking. She heard one of them say, "Yeah, we showed him, didn't we!" which was followed by a lot of giggling. One of the girls in the group was Maggie's friend Lauren.

Later on, Maggie asked Lauren what the girls had been talking about. Lauren made Maggie promise not to tell anybody what she was about to tell her. Some of the girls had gotten together and made up the story about Mr. Johnson so that he would get in trouble and have to leave the school. Maggie did not like Mr. Johnson because she felt he was unfair to females, but she did not think it was right for him to lose his job and have to go around with this label of being guilty of sexual harassment. Lauren was a good friend of Maggie's, and she did not want her to get in trouble. Also, the girls in the school could gang up on a person and be very mean when they were thwarted (as Mr. Johnson found out).

Discussion Questions:

1) Should Maggie protect her friend (and herself) by concealing the story, or should she risk social ostracism by helping a teacher that she did not even like?

2) What other avenues were open to Maggie and her friends?

3) Discuss the seriousness of a sexual harassment charge.

4) Which should have more value in this case, justice or friendship?

We have discussed this Tough Choice.

_____   _____
Parent/Guardian Signature   Student Signature

SEXUALITY DILEMMA #2

Jenny's best friend Rachel has been dating Ben for about two months. Rachel thinks he is the greatest. She swears he can do no wrong. He does seem perfect to Jenny, too. One Saturday morning, Rachel starts crying the moment she sees Jenny. Jenny cannot even speculate as to why she is upset. Eventually, after much encouragement, Rachel begins to talk. Jenny comes to find out that Rachel had sex with her boyfriend the night before. Jenny does not think that Rachel wanted to, though. Rachel won't say that he raped her, but Jenny can tell that the event wasn't exactly consensual. Rachel is blaming herself because she thinks she led him on by the way she was acting. She said that she had been putting up resistance and really didn't want to have sex. But they had been drinking and she says that some memories are a little fuzzy. Jenny wants her to tell someone about it so she can get help. Rachel doesn't want to. She says Ben didn't mean to do anything wrong. She doesn't want Jenny to tell anybody about it either. Rachel doesn't want anyone to know what happened. She doesn't want her boyfriend in trouble and she says she will never forgive Jenny if she tells anyone. Jenny knows Rachel needs help—that what happened wasn't right—but she doesn't want to put her friend through more grief or go against her wishes. Jenny is the only one who knows about this.

Discussion Questions:

1) What should Jenny do?

2) What ramifications will her action have? Her inaction?

3) What do you think will happen to Ben if Jenny tells an adult in authority about what happened? What will happen to Rachel?

4) Is this situation worth putting a friendship in jeopardy?

We have discussed this Tough Choice.

_____   _____

Parent/Guardian Signature   Student Signature

SEXUALITY DILEMMA #3

Janet and Shannon share the same beliefs about premarital sex. So much so that they both came to an agreement four years ago that each of them would help to make sure the other would keep the commitment by taking steps to ensure that the other would not put themselves in a bad situation. But since that time, Janet has been getting pretty serious with the person she is dating. She confides in Shannon that she plans on having sex this weekend. When Shannon tries to bring up the agreement they had, Janet says that she knows what the two of them promised but assures Shannon that this is a totally different situation. Janet appreciates that Shannon cares, but says that the agreement was originally intended for a situation where one of them was having sexual feelings for a person that they really did not know. Janet confesses that this is "true love" and wants to share this love with sexual intimacy with her boyfriend. Further, she tells Shannon that she has never been more sure of anything, seems very happy and very sure of her decision, and would like Shannon to be happy for her.

Discussion Questions:

1) What should Shannon do?

2) Should either of the girls' parents be told?

3) How can present emotions overshadow lifelong beliefs?

4) What does "being a friend" truly mean in this situation?

We have discussed this Tough Choice.

_____   _____

Parent/Guardian Signature   Student Signature

SEXUALITY DILEMMA #4

Jenny and Ashley are best friends. They have grown up together and have gone to school together their entire lives. The great thing about their relationship is they can share things with each other that they cannot tell anybody else. They are extremely similar in their interests. The only difference is that Ashley is sexually active and Jenny has decided to wait until marriage before having sex. One Saturday morning, Jenny stops by Ashley's house. Jenny is anxious to hear about the details of the previous night's party, which she could not attend due to a family commitment. She enters Ashley's room and sees her friend crying on the bed. When she asks Ashley what is wrong, Ashley tells her that she made a mistake last night. She does not want to share any more information but Jenny presses the issue because she knows Ashley wants to tell somebody about what happened. Ashley finally relents and explains that at the party she had been drinking and talking with Scott, their mutual friend. Ashley and Scott decided to be "alone," so they went to one of the unoccupied bedrooms and began making out. Ashley tells Jenny that after a while, she wanted to stop and return to the party, but Scott wanted to continue. When she resisted, Scott became forceful. She tried to stop him, but eventually they had sex. Ashley ended the story by saying repeatedly, "It's all my fault." It became pretty clear to Jenny that Ashley had been raped, but when she suggested this to Ashley, Ashley said, "Oh no, Scott would never do that, and I shouldn't have been there in the first place." She then asks Jenny to promise that she will not tell anyone.

Discussion Questions:

1) What should Jenny do?

2) Whom should be contacted? What steps should be taken?

3) Does it matter if Ashley and Scott had had a sexual encounter in the past?

4) How would you respond to somebody who claims that the victim is partly to blame in a rape situation?

5) What could have been done to prevent this situation from occurring?

We have discussed this Tough Choice.

_____   _____

Parent/Guardian Signature   Student Signature

SEXUALITY DILEMMA #5

   Jill and Matt are good friends who both work as counselors for a church camp. They carpool to work, each one alternating weeks to drive. One day, during Jill's week of driving, Jill stops to pick up Matt but discovers her friend asleep. Matt apologizes and asks if Jill would mind waiting fifteen minutes while he showers and gets dressed. Jill says okay and asks Matt if she can check her email on Matt's computer while she is waiting. Matt has no problem with this, so Jill sits down at his computer. On Jill's home computer, she has her email server's web address bookmarked so she can get to her email messages quicker. By force of habit, she checks Matt's bookmarked section. What she sees stops her dead in her tracks. Listed on Matt's bookmarked page are a handful of web addresses for sites featuring pornographic pictures. Considering where they work, this causes Jill to feel uncomfortable. However, she cannot believe her friend would be interested in such material and is sure that there must be another reason the sites are bookmarked on his computer.

Discussion Questions:

1) What should Jill do?

2) How can a person's private life affect their professional life? Why or why not?

3) Is Internet pornography different than traditional forms of pornography (magazines, books, videos, etc.)? Why or why not?

4) Is pornography a private matter or does it affect a larger part of society?

We have discussed this Tough Choice.

_____   _____

Parent/Guardian Signature   Student Signature

Notes

1. "When Teens Have Sex: Issues and Trends," 1999. A KIDS COUNT Special Report, The Annie E. Casey Foundation, 701 St. Paul Street, Baltimore, MD 21202.

2. K. A. Moore, A. K. Driscoll, and L. D. Lindberg (1998). *A Statistical Portrait of Adolescent Sex, Contraception, and Childbearing* (Washington, D.C.: The National Campaign to Prevent Teen Pregnancy, 1998).

3. American Association of University Women, "Hostile Hallways: The AAUW Survey on Sexual Harassment in America's Schools," 1993.

4. Patricia Hersch, *A Tribe Apart: A Journey Into the Heart of American Adolescence* (The Ballantine Publishing Group, 1998) 64–65.

5. Statistics from: Robin Warshaw, *I Never Called it Rape*. (Perennial, 1994).

6. http://www.callrape.com/vic-help.htm

7. http://familydoctor.org/handouts/314.html

8. Analysis of S. K. Henshaw, *U.S. Teenage Pregnancy Statistics* (New York: Alan Guttmacher Institute, May 1996); and J.D. Forest *Proportion of U.S. Women Pregnant Before Age 20* (New York: Alan Guttmacher Institute, 1986, unpublished).

9. S. K. Henshaw, "Unintended Pregnancy in the United States," *Family Planning Perspectives* 30(no. 1): 24-29 & 46. Table 1.

10. R. A. Maynard, ed. *Kids Having Kids: A Robin Hood Foundation Special Report on the Costs of Adolescent Childbearing*, (New York: Robin Hood Foundation, 1996).

11. B. Wolfe and M. Perozek "Teen Children's Health and Health Care Use," R. A. Maynard, ed., *Kids Having Kids: Economic Costs and Social Consequences of Teen Pregnancy*, (Washington, D.C.: The Urban Institute Press, 1997): 181–203.

12. R. A. Maynard, ed., *Kids Having Kids*.

13. R. M. George and B. J. Lee "Abuse and Neglect of Children," 1997. R. A. Maynard, ed., *Kids Having Kids: Economic Costs and Social Consequences of Teen Pregnancy* (Washington, D.C.: The Urban Institute Press, 1997): 205–230.

14. Alan Guttmacher Institute, *Sex and America's Teenagers* (New York: Alan Guttmacher Institute, 1994) p. 38.

15. National Institute of Allergy and Infectious Diseases—National Institutes of Health "Sexually Transmitted Diseases" (autumn 1998).

16. The Alan Guttmacher Institute, "Facts in Brief: Teen Sex and Pregnancy," 1998.

17. Ibid.

18. http://www.pregnancyresources.org/STD.html

19. Ibid.

20. P. Donovan *Testing Positive: Sexually Transmitted Disease and the Public Health Response* (New York: Alan Guttmacher Institute, 1993): 24.

21. World Health Organization, December 1997 Fact Sheet, available at: http://www.who.ch/

22. http://www.pregnancyresources.org/STD.html

23. National Vital Statistics Reports, 47, no. 9, June 30, 1999.

24. Planned Parenthood Federation of America, Inc., 1999. Found at: http://www.plannedparenthood.org/TEENISSUES/BCCHOICES/BCCHOICES.HTML

25. EDK Associates for *Seventeen* magazine and the Ms. Foundation for Women. *Teenagers Under Pressure*, 1996.

26. K. A. Moore, et al. *A Statistical Portrait of Adolescent Sex, Contraception, and Child Bearing*, (Washington, D.C.: National Campaign to Prevent Teen Pregnancy, 1998) 11.

27. Ibid.

28. EDK Associates for *Seventeen* magazine and the Ms. Foundation for Women, *Teenagers Under Pressure*, 1996.

29. K. L. Graves and B. C. Leigh, "The relationship of substance use to sexual activity among young adults in the United States," *Family Planning Perspectives* (1995) 27: 18–22.

30. D. P. Orr, M. Beiter, and G. Ingersoll, "Premature sexual activity as an indicator of psychosocial risk," *Pediatrics*, 87, no. 2 (1 February 1991) 141–147.

31. M. D. Resnick,. P. S. Bearman, R. W. Blum, et al. "Protecting adolescents from harm: findings from the National Longitudinal Study on Adolescent Health," *JAMA* 278 (1997): 823–832.

32. Princeton Survey Research Associates for the Henry J. Kaiser Family Foundation, *The 1996 Kaiser Family Foundation Survey on Teens and Sex: Why Teens Today Say They Need to Know, and Who They Listen To* (Menlo Park, CA: Author, June 1996).

33. Princeton Survey Research Associates for the National Campaign to Prevent Teen Pregnancy, "A Review of Public Opinion About Teen Pregnancy," (Washington, D.C.: Author, September, 1996).

34. Women's Sports Foundation *Report: Sport and Teen Pregnancy* (New York: The Women's Sports Foundation, 1998).

35. Who's Who Among High School Students, *22nd Annual Survey of High Achievers: Attitudes and Opinions from the Nation's High Achieving Teens*. (Lake Forest, IL: Educational Communications, 1991).

36. M. D. Resnick,. P. S. Bearman, R. W. Blum, et al. "Protecting adolescents from harm: findings from the National Longitudinal Study on Adolescent Health,"*JAMA* 278 (1997).

SUICIDE
SUICIDE
SUICIDE
SUICIDE
SUICIDE
SUICIDE

SUICIDE

SUICIDE
SUICIDE
SUICIDE
SUICIDE
SUICIDE
SUICIDE
SUICIDE
SUICIDE
SUICIDE
SUICIDE
SUICIDE
SUICIDE
SUICIDE
SUICIDE
SUICIDE
SUICIDE

Overview of Suicide Issues • • • • • • • • • • •

- ## What is suicide and what causes it?

  Suicide is the deliberate taking of one's own life. There is no single cause for suicide. Usually it is the combination of many factors. Among the reasons individuals may consider suicide are: feelings of loneliness, loss of a loved one, loss of income or independence, declining health, divorce, relationship break-up, drug and alcohol addiction, unanticipated failure or rejection, and questioning of self-worth.

- ## Are thoughts of suicide common in teenagers? Why?

  One simply needs to look at the changes young people are experiencing to understand why thoughts of suicide are common among teenagers.[1] Childhood ties to parents are loosened, a new sense of independence is felt, teenagers seek their own individuality, and they discover their emerging sexuality and identity. At this time, these new experiences can lead them away from the habits and security of their childhood lives. Facing two different lives, adolescents are pulled in each direction, causing anxiety and emotional distress that frustrates them and those closest to them. When trying to resolve such conflicting demands, adolescents often develop impulsive behaviors. The combination of letting go of past experiences while facing an uncertain future causes adolescents to question their identity, leading to self-doubt, feelings of inferiority, and loneliness. There may be pressure or criticism from families or friends, traumatic experiences, or struggles to discover one's niche, leading to perceptions of a lack of love, place, or worth. Teenagers may become depressed, yet not have life experience to know the reasons for their pain. In times like these, extreme measures may be taken simply as a means of regaining control. Unfortunately, suicide is sometimes incorrectly seen as such a means.

- ## How is depression related to suicide?

  Often feelings of depression are associated with those thinking about or attempting suicide. Depression affects one's ability to function on a daily basis and one's relationships with others. Depression is a serious mood disorder and medical condition that should not be confused with feeling blue for a couple days. Depression is a complex medical and psychological condition that involves a chemical imbalance in the brain. According to the National Institute of Mental Health, there may be a biological link between depression and suicide. Although nothing definitive has been discovered, some research has shown that both depressed people and those who have committed suicide have lower-than-normal levels of serotonin in their brains.[2] Serotonin is a neurotransmitter that inhibits self-harm. But regardless of such research, the despair that a depressed person feels may make it easier for thoughts of suicide to develop in a person's mind. However, it should be noted that not all suicidal people are depressed, and most depressed people never consider suicide.

- ## How common are suicides? How common are suicides among teenagers?

  In 1999, suicide took the lives of 29,199 people in the United States.[3] This figure is larger than the number of people killed by homicides. Overall, suicide is the eleventh leading cause of death for people in this country.[4] Males are four times more likely to die from suicide than females,[5] but females are more likely to attempt suicide than males.[6] Some people try repeatedly to commit suicide.

  Suicide is the third leading cause of death for young people aged fifteen to twenty-four.[7] Almost 14 percent of all suicides were by people under the age of 25.[8] In 1999, more teenagers and young adults died from suicide than from AIDS, heart disease, cancer, birth defects, strokes, and chronic lung disease combined.[9] Studies indicate that 24.1 percent of high school students had thought seriously about attempting suicide, 17.7 percent had made a specific plan to attempt suicide, and 8.7 percent had attempted suicide.[10]

  To learn more about the issues surrounding suicide, the National Institute of Mental Health offers detailed answers to a wide variety of questions. You can locate this information at http://www.nimh.nih.gov/research/suicidefaq.cfm.

- ## What should be done for a friend who is considering suicide?

According to David L. Conroy. Ph.D., there are several steps that should be taken when speaking with someone, either in person or by phone, who is thinking about committing suicide.[11] These steps include:

Be yourself. There are no "right" words. Your voice will convey your concern.

Listen. Giving the person an opportunity to unload his or her feelings is a positive sign, regardless of how negative the tone of the conversation is. Also, simply talking about their problems will give suicidal people relief from their loneliness and pent-up feelings. In addition, as they continue to talk and get tired, their body chemistry changes, perhaps taking the edge off any agitated state.

Do not judge. Be sympathetic, calm, and accepting. Avoid arguments, giving advice, or making the person feel as if they have to justify their feelings.

If the person mentions that they don't think they can go on, ask the question, "Are you having thoughts of committing suicide?" Contrary to certain myths, the mention of suicide is not putting thoughts into this person's head. You are conveying how serious your concern is, and that it is alright for this person to share their feelings with you.

If the answer to the question is "yes," begin to ask further questions: "Have you thought how you would do it?" "Have you got what you need?" "Have you thought about when you would do it?" Nearly 95 percent of all suicidal callers will answer "no" to one of these questions or reveal that the time is set for some time in the future. This will be a relief to both you and the other person.

Other suggestions are:[12]

Take it seriously. More than 75 percent of all people who completed suicides indicated to others that they were in deep despair or contemplating suicide before they followed through on it.

Remember: suicidal behavior is a cry for help. A suicidal person is ambivalent about life. Part of the person wants to remain alive and part of the person wants to die to end the suffering. Calling or talking to another person comes from the part of the person that wants to remain alive. He or she probably views you as someone they greatly respect or who he or she feels is compassionate and might be able to help.

No secrets. The person may instruct you not to tell anyone what they have told you, but remember, this is a cry for help. Do not try to do it alone.

Urge professional help. If the person is truly suicidal do not leave them alone. But in any case, being patient, yet persistent, in sorting out the options for the person is the best thing for them. Let the person know you want to maintain contact.

An extremely helpful website that was constructed specifically for individuals who were having thoughts of suicide is http://www.metanoia.org/suicide. A national emergency contact number is:

1-800-784-2433 (1-800-SUICIDE)

For contact information in each state, visit: http://suicidehotlines.com.

Church Teaching on Suicide • • • • • • • • •

- **What is the Catholic Church's position on suicide?**
  The Catholic Church is unequivocally against suicide. It is contrary to the fifth commandment ("Thou shall not kill"). The *Catechism of the Catholic Church* states: "Suicide contradicts the natural inclination of the human being to preserve and perpetuate his life. It is gravely contrary to the just love of self. It likewise offends love of neighbor because it unjustly breaks the ties of solidarity with family, nation, and other human societies to which we continue to have obligations. Suicide is contrary to love for the living God" (2281).

- **Why is that the position of the Catholic Church?**
  The Church teaches that God is the owner of our lives and bodies: "We are stewards, not owners, of the life God has entrusted to us. It is not ours to dispose of" (*CCC*, 2280).

- **Will someone who commits suicide go to hell?**
  No one knows the answer to questions like this except God himself. The Church does teach that grave psychological disturbance, anguish, or grave fear of hardship, suffering, or torture can diminish the responsibility of the one committing suicide. God alone judges these persons and can provide the opportunity for repentance.

- **Which Scripture passages are relevant to the issue of suicide?**
  Old Testament

  Genesis 3:5

  Deuteronomy 32:39

  1 Samuel 2:6

  Wisdom 16:13

  New Testament

  I Corinthians 6:19–20

- **What can I do to help prevent suicide?**
  Here are four ideas for you to consider:

    1. Pray.
    2. Have strong, open communication with God, family, and friends about this topic. Talking through problems and praying to God will do immeasurable good.
    3. Be aware of family and friends, especially in times of crisis (e.g., death of a loved one, break up of a relationship). It is in these times that your family member or friend needs you. Be there for them.
    4. Be aware of warning signs including depression, talk of suicide, and someone who is exhibiting unusual behavior (e. g., giving away their possessions).

SUICIDE DILEMMA #1

Some people just don't stand out in a crowd. David was this type of person. He was very quiet, keeping to himself most of the time. Students in the school thought he was a little strange but generally left him alone. One group of students, however, constantly made David the subject of their jokes. David never had a response, he simply kept his head down and remained quiet.

Sean was good friends with several of the kids in this group of teasers. Overall, Sean was a good person. He was very involved at his school, from athletics to student government, and even found time to perform charity work on the side. But when his friends would make fun of David, he felt compelled to join in, but not with the same intensity. He really did not want to make fun of David, but he also did not want to go against what his friends were doing.

One Friday, Sean was at the library when David suddenly appeared and sat down at his table. Sean was surprised, but the look on David's face forced him to remain seated. It was a look of pain and fear that Sean had never seen before. Sean asked David what was wrong, and that was all it took. He told Sean that he wanted to talk to him because he seemed like a leader and a person who would listen. He described to Sean how painful it was to be an outsider and not part of the "in" crowd. He went on to explain that he suffered from depression, and even went so far as to confide that he had considered suicide a year ago. Sean was touched that David had chosen him as a confidante. David continued talking, as if he had not spoken to another person in years, and Sean soon realized that they had several common interests and that he enjoyed talking with David. He felt awful for ever having made fun of David and promised himself that it would not happen again.

Later that day, Sean was standing with his friends, hurriedly packing his books in order to catch the team bus for the football when David came up to him again. His friends immediately began making fun of David but fell silent when David began talking to Sean. David looked completely upset and indicated that something terrible had happened. Then David looked intently at Sean and said emphatically, "Goodbye Sean." Sean had to catch the bus, but given the subject of their earlier conversation, he was worried about David.

Discussion Questions:

1) What should Sean do?

2) Would the situation be different if Sean knew David better?

3) Have you ever known somebody like David? How was he treated?

4) What steps could be taken to make sure David doesn't feel like an outsider?

We have discussed this Tough Choice.

_____
Parent/Guardian Signature

_____
Student Signature

SUICIDE DILEMMA #2

Kent is a loner at school. He feels like he has no friends and people often walk by him as if he doesn't exist. The popular crowd has even teased him and he has come to resent them. Sometimes Kent wishes he could just disappear or make everyone else disappear. Thoughts of suicide have crossed his mind, but he feels as if he has no one to turn to for support. He has contemplated revenge against the popular crowd, but he remembers what happened at Columbine and other high schools and cannot imagine doing such harm. Kent feels confused, helpless, afraid, depressed, and angry.

Discussion Questions:

1) What should Kent do?

2) What options does he have for seeking help?

3) What can society do to prevent such tragedies as suicide and school shootings?

4) Have you ever felt depressed? If so, how did you get through it?

5) If you were Kent's friend, what would you do?

6) If you barely knew Kent, what could you do?

We have discussed this Tough Choice.

_____

Parent/Guardian Signature

_____

Student Signature

Notes

1. http://jaring.my/befrienders/youth1.htm

2. http://www.nimh.nih.gov/research/suicidefaq.cfm

3. NCHS National Vital Statistics System for numbers of deaths, U.S. Bureau of Census for population estimates. Statistics compiled using WISQARS™ produced by the Office of Statistics and Programming, NCIPC, CDC.

4. Ibid.

5. Ibid.

6. *Suicide and Life Threatening Behavior* 28 no. 1 (1998): 1–23.

7. NCHS National Vital Statistics System for numbers of deaths, U.S. Bureau of Census for population estimates.

8. Ibid.

9. Ibid.

10. Centers for Disease Control (CDC), "Youth Risk Behavior Surveillance—United States, 1995". *MMWR*; 45, no. SS-4, (1996): 1–86. Also found at http://www.dianedew.com/suistats.htm

11. http://www.metanoia.org/suicide/sphone.htm

12. http://www.metanoia.org/suicide/whattodo.htm

OTHER DILEMMAS

GOVERNMENT DILEMMA #1

Congressman Frank Dillard has been a hard-working representative for his district for fifteen years. He has a very good reputation among his constituency as well as other representatives. The House of Representatives has proposed a bill that would put many restrictions on the tobacco industry. Congressman Dillard has strong feelings about the dangers of tobacco since his father died of emphysema at a young age. However, the district that Congressman Dillard has lived in all his life and now represents is a major tobacco-producing district. Congressman Dillard's constituency is comprised of many tobacco farmers whose incomes rely on a strong tobacco market. Congressman Dillard is torn between his personal beliefs and his constituency's desires.

Discussion Questions:

1) Should Congressman Dillard follow his personal beliefs or the wishes of his constituents?

2) Does Congressman Dillard have a moral obligation to vote the way his constituents want him to since he represents them?

3) Does Congressman Dillard have a moral obligation to go against his constituents because he knows the dangers of tobacco?

We have discussed this Tough Choice.

_____   _____

Parent/Guardian Signature   Student Signature

GOVERNMENT DILEMMA #2

Brian, 25, has recently completed law school. His first job is as a public defense lawyer who works with those who have allegedly committed grave crimes. Most of these "criminals" are underprivileged and have led very tough lives. One of the reasons why Brian chose this work is so that he can defend those who have been victims of poverty and difficult situations.

Brian's first client is assigned to him by the court. The man has been accused of murder. He does not admit to either doing or not doing the crime. He asks Brian to base his defense on casting "reasonable doubt." Brian, meanwhile, is not sold on the man's innocence. Brian thinks he could win the trial and is anxious to get started with his law career, but he's not sure whether he can justify defending a man who is very likely guilty of a brutal crime.

Discussion Questions:

1) What should Brian do?

2) What if the crime was not murder? Would it make a difference if the crime was theft, arson, or cheating on taxes?

3) What comes first in your life: money, law, or your ideals?

4) Can you separate your personal life beliefs from your professional life beliefs?

5) Would you be able to work in the type of profession that Brian does? Why or why not?

We have discussed this Tough Choice.

_____   _____

Parent/Guardian Signature   Student Signature

MULTICULTURAL DILEMMA #1

Kim lives in a predominantly white neighborhood. Theresa is one of only five black students in a student body of five hundred. Kim and Theresa are not friends but have a few classes together. One day, Kim gets to school and learns that Theresa was pulled over at night and unfairly harassed and physically assaulted by two white policemen. It makes the front page of the newspaper and everyone is talking about it at school. From all the published reports, the police were out of line in their use of force and many believe the assault was racially motivated. Plans are made in the community for a protest, blockading the outside of the police station. The chief of police has stated that while demonstrations are permitted by law, any demonstration that impedes the normal routine of the police force will be treated as an obstruction of justice. Classmates of the girls are planning on leaving school during their fourth and fifth periods to protest at the police station. Kim is considering going to the protest as well.

Discussion Questions:

1) What should Kim do?

2) What could be the consequences for going to the protest?

3) What is your responsibility in promoting racial harmony and justice?

4) How should one respond to unjust actions?

5) Is acting on the behalf of justice a reason for skipping school?

We have discussed this Tough Choice.

_____

Parent/Guardian Signature

_____

Student Signature

MULTICULTURAL DILEMMA #2

Mark's English class is reading a story about the Holocaust. To further the students' understanding, Mark's teacher, Mr. Davis, brings in a guest lecturer. This guest speaker is an older man who was part of the "Nazi Youth" while growing up in Germany in the 1930s. The first part of the talk is extremely informative and delivered well. But about thirty minutes into the lecture, the speaker begins to espouse anti-Semitic views, some implicit, others more explicit. He makes comments that offend Mark and with which Mark vehemently disagrees. Mr. Davis told the class before the lecture that questions and comments were appropriate any time.

Discussion Questions:

1) Should Mark raise his hand and tell the speaker he is offended by his remarks?

2) What would be the consequences if Mark chooses to speak up?

3) What if the consequence for confronting the speaker was suspension from school? Should Mark still speak up?

4) How important is it to stand up for what you believe in?

5) How do you stand up for your beliefs?

We have discussed this Tough Choice.

_____   _____
Parent/Guardian Signature   Student Signature

MULTICULTURAL DILEMMA #3

Ashley and some of her friends are hanging out at the mall watching people and talking. Comments are constantly being made about the different people they see:

"He walks like a girl. He must be gay."

"That guy's huge! I bet he uses steroids."

"Did you see that girl? What a nerd! Her hair is greasy and her outfit's atrocious."

"Don't play country music in this crowd. Too many African Americans here."

Ashley is uncomfortable with the comments being made, but she does not say anything.

Discussion Questions:

1) What should Ashley do?

2) What is a stereotype? Name some of the stereotypes you know.

3) How do stereotypes affect people?

4) How should you react if someone defined you by a stereotype? (For example, if you were tall, people assume you play basketball.)

5) Why are stereotypes used so often in our society?

6) How does the media—television, movies, music, magazines—affect our stereotypes?

7) When have you used stereotypes? How did the other person react?

We have discussed this Tough Choice.

_____

Parent/Guardian Signature

_____

Student Signature

MULTICULTURAL DILEMMA #4

Timoteo was excited. Tonight he had a date with Shakema. Both are sophomores at the same high school and had been friends for a long time, but now they were ready to start dating. While walking down the stairs, his mom asks if he could come into the living room to talk with her and his dad. His parents sit him down, and his father says, "Your mother and I agree. We do not approve of you going on this date with Shakema."

This surprises Timoteo, and he asks, "Why not? You already know her. I know you like her." His mother responds, "That was before. She makes a nice friend. We do not approve of the dating." Timoteo asks again, "Why?" His father said, "She's black. You are Filipino. We do not approve."

Discussion Questions:

1) What should Timoteo do?

2) Should Timoteo tell Shakema what his parents said?

3) How would you react if your parents approached you with a similar situation?

4) How would you react if your date's parents disapproved of you the way Timoteo's parents disapproved of Shakema?

5) How does your peer group react towards interracial dating?

We have discussed this Tough Choice.

_____   _____

Parent/Guardian Signature   Student Signature

PARENT-CHILD DILEMMA #1

Shelley's best friend, LaDonna, has not been getting along with her parents lately. Each day, it seems, La Donna recounts a new story of a fight that occurred between herself and her parents the previous night. LaDonna constantly complains about how strict they are and how they do not understand her. They never let her go out and if she gets any grade less than an A, they are outraged. Once, LaDonna came home with an 85 percent on a test and her parents grounded her for a week. LaDonna believes that this is negatively affecting her personal, social, emotional, and spiritual well-being. She confides in Shelley that she cannot take it anymore and is going to run away from home the next weekend.

Discussion Questions:

1) What should Shelley advise LaDonna to do?

2) Should Shelley feel obligated to tell LaDonna's parents?

3) What other options does Shelley have?

4) What could have been done to avoid this situation?

We have discussed this Tough Choice.

_____

Parent/Guardian Signature

_____

Student Signature

PARENT-CHILD DILEMMA #2

Tom and Erik are high school sophomores and are huge fans of the same rock band. Between them they know every song the band plays. Tom's mother has been supportive of his guitar playing because it is a hobby that he is passionate about, but she is concerned about the drug culture she believes surrounds the band. Tom is introspective and spends most of his time playing music in his room.

Tom and Erik learn that the band they like is playing at an area arena the following weekend. Tom's mother forbids him to attend the concert because she knows that there will be illegal substances there. On the night of the concert, Tom tells his mother that he is sleeping over at Erik's house. The boys now have an opportunity to go to the concert.

Discussion Questions:

1) Should Tom attend the concert against his mother's wishes?

2) What advice would you give him as a friend?

3) How might Tom convince his mother to let him go to the concert?

We have discussed this Tough Choice.

_____   _____

Parent/Guardian Signature   Student Signature

PARENT-CHILD DILEMMA #3

Frank has a wife and two small children. He was laid off from his job at a chemical plant four months ago and has not been able to find work since. Because of the loss in family income, he and his family could no longer afford the apartment they had been renting. They were forced to move somewhere they could afford, which happened to be in an area of town with a high crime and burglary rate. Frank finds a job as a night watchman at an office building, but that means leaving his family alone for most nights. He is afraid to do so in such an unsafe neighborhood. When he asks his new neighbors about how they protect their families, they all tell him that the only true way to protect loved ones is by purchasing a gun. Frank wants to ensure his family's safety but he does not like the idea of keeping a gun in the house.

Discussion Questions:

1) What should Frank do?

2) What are the dangers of keeping firearms in the home?

3) Are there any alternatives to protecting a family?

4) If a gun is deemed necessary, what precautions should be taken to ensure it is used safely?

We have discussed this Tough Choice.

_____   _____

Parent/Guardian Signature   Student Signature

POVERTY DILEMMA #1

Emily works as a computer consultant in Boston. She is single and earns a very generous salary. Today on her way to lunch she passes a man who claims to be homeless. He is sitting in front of a grocery store and begs her for money. The only money she is carrying is a $20 bill and some loose change. She wants to help the man, but she is not sure what he will spend the money on.

Discussion Questions:

1) What should Emily do?

2) Does it matter how old the man is, what the man looks like, or what gender the person is?

3) Does Emily's income matter?

4) What options does Emily have other than giving money?

We have discussed this Tough Choice.

_____   _____
Parent/Guardian Signature   Student Signature

POVERTY DILEMMA #2

Over the school break Tracy's mom graciously provides her with the opportunity to fly to visit her friend Chris in Los Angeles. Her week has been wonderfully spent seeing the sites of southern California. The last day of her stay they are to visit the Los Angeles art museum. As she drives with Chris from the outskirts of LA further into the heart of the city, she passes through some rundown neighborhoods. In the heat of midday, children are running up and down the street, involved in a fast game of street baseball. Teenagers are relaxing, huddled around cars and chatting with one another. Mothers are found clustered in groups, tending to the toddlers, recalling their morning to one another.

Tracy is immediately caught up in the vitality of the street activity, mesmerized by this vibrant community of families who really seem to know one another and freely share their lives with each other. She is so enthralled that when Chris off-handedly interrupts her thoughts with a scornful comment, she is shocked. Chris says: "This could be a nice area if these people would only take care of it. Look at all that graffiti."

Discussion Questions:

1) How should Tracy respond to Chris's statement?

2) What could Tracy do, if anything, to help broaden the minds of people like Chris?

We have discussed this Tough Choice.

_____

Parent/Guardian Signature

_____

Student Signature

RELATIONSHIP DILEMMA #1

Jackie is a senior in high school. She has a very close friend, Lindsey, who has been dating the same guy for the past year. Jackie has noticed in the past few months, however, that Lindsey's boyfriend has been controlling much of Lindsey's life. For example, her boyfriend bought Lindsey a cell phone so that he would be able to contact her whenever he wanted. Lindsey has not been able to spend much time with Jackie lately because she seems to always be with her boyfriend. In addition, Lindsey's grades are starting to decline, and Jackie is worried that she might not graduate. She also notices that Lindsey has been arguing more frequently with her parents.

Discussion Questions:

1) What should Jackie do?

2) If you were in Lindsey's place, what would you want a friend to tell you?

3) Whom should she speak to or approach first?

4) What can be done to avoid being caught in possessive relationships?

We have discussed this Tough Choice.

_____

Parent/Guardian Signature

_____

Student Signature

RELATIONSHIP DILEMMA #2

Scott has known Dan since they were five years old and they have been great friends ever since. Scott has known Christine for three years and has become very close to her as well. Scott thinks the world of both of them. So much so, that a year and a half ago, Scott introduced the two of them. Dan and Christine took a liking to each other and have been dating ever since. One Friday night, Scott attends a party where a lot of his friends are celebrating the end of another week of school. He is unfamiliar with the house he is in and needs to find a bathroom. He opens up one door after another, but none of them is a bathroom. Scott tries one last door at the end of the hall, and when he opens it, he sees Dan and a girl he does not know kissing on a bed. Dan sees Scott, and his face goes white as Scott quickly closes the door. All weekend Scott thinks about what to do. When he comes to school on Monday, Dan says he needs to talk with him. When they are alone, Dan tells Scott that he and Christine have been having problems recently. He says they are both unsure about their relationship and where it is. He asks Scott not to tell Christine about Friday night because he has to sort some things out. Scott is not sure if this means Dan will talk to Christine about the situation himself or not.

Discussion Questions:

1) What should Scott do?

2) If Dan doesn't talk to Christine, should Scott do anything?

3) To whom does Scott have more allegiance?

4) Are male/male or female/female friendships more important than male/female friendships?

5) If this happens again, is Scott absolutely obligated to do something?

We have discussed this Tough Choice.

_____

Parent/Guardian Signature

_____

Student Signature

RELATIONSHIP DILEMMA #3

James and Hope have been dating for two and a half years. They have talked of getting married. Hope knows that James relies on her and that she is an enormous part of his life. She sometimes worries his life may fall apart without her. But now she feels herself growing distant from James. She doesn't want to bring this up to him for fear of hurting him, though she would like to find a way to break up. James has no knowledge of her confusion.

Discussion Questions:

1) What should Hope do?

2) Are relationships healthy if one individual is completely dependent on another?

3) What is a charitable way to break up with somebody?

We have discussed this Tough Choice.

_____

Parent/Guardian Signature

_____

Student Signature

RELATIONSHIP DILEMMA #4

Jason and Michael are seniors on the varsity football team. They have been friends since freshman year. Michael has been dating Jason's sister Rene for about six months. During a conversation in the locker room one afternoon the players are talking about cheating on their girlfriends. Most of the guys don't think it is wrong as long as they don't get caught. Michael echoes the sentiment of the group by arguing that, "if nobody else knows, how can it be wrong?"

Jason has noticed that Michael has been hanging out with the captain of the cheerleading squad before school. When Jason approaches Michael about the topic, Michael becomes defensive and says that they are just friends.

Discussion Questions:

1) Should Jason tell Rene about the locker room conversation?

2) Should Jason confront Michael about this topic again?

3) What is Jason's responsibility as a teammate? As a brother?

4) Should Jason tell his parents what he has heard?

We have discussed this Tough Choice.

_____

Parent/Guardian Signature

_____

Student Signature

RELATIONSHIP DILEMMA #5

John and Amy have been going out for three months. John is intellectual and funny, while Amy is sensitive and beautiful. The fact that his girlfriend is extremely attractive, until recently, was something John was happy about. But in the past few weeks, John has been noticing that whenever the two of them go out, guys are constantly hitting on Amy. John completely trusts Amy, and he does not want to bring up the subject with her because he does not want to appear jealous. The main object of John's concern is Vince, the captain of the football team. He constantly flirts with Amy in school, and John has heard from friends that Vince said he "doesn't care if Amy has a boyfriend because she'll be mine soon." Tonight, John and Amy are at a party and once again, Vince appears to be monopolizing Amy's time. John tries to ignore it but he notices Vince touch Amy's waist and hands on repeated occasions. One of John's friends tells him that Vince promised he would "have" Amy by the end of the night.

Discussion Questions:

1) What should John do?

2) Whom should John approach?

3) What are effective ways to communicate feeling uncomfortable in a relationship?

4) Are there any accepted norms of behavior for situations like this?

We have discussed this Tough Choice.

_____

Parent/Guardian Signature

_____

Student Signature

SCIENCE & MEDICINE DILEMMA #1

Sarah is a high school senior and works in an AIDS clinic as a nurse's aid. She wants to be a doctor someday and has spent her last two summers working at this clinic. Sarah respects the code of confidentiality that her patients require and recognizes the social stigmas that are unfairly attached to AIDS. Sarah is also very careful to take appropriate steps of safety when dealing with patients. This includes wearing latex gloves, a facemask, and occasionally goggles. One afternoon while shopping at the mall with friends, Sarah encounters a patient from the clinic shopping alone. They pass each other and smile politely. While shopping in the store, Sarah hears a commotion in the back of the store. She follows the noise to a crowd of people where all the attention is focused and sees the woman from the clinic passed out on the floor. A man steps forward and says that he knows CPR. He asks everyone to back up so he can begin to help the woman.

Discussion Questions:

1) Should Sarah tell the man that this woman has AIDS?

2) Does she have a greater responsibility to the patient or to the helpful stranger?

3) Does it matter that the man's children are watching?

4) What if the woman is bleeding from the mouth?

5) In what cases should confidentiality be compromised?

We have discussed this Tough Choice.

_____   _____

Parent/Guardian Signature   Student Signature

SCIENCE & MEDICINE DILEMMA #2

Maureen is a doctor in the emergency room at the local hospital. On a particularly quiet night, the hospital receives word that there has been a horrible accident only a few blocks away. It seems that a car ran a red light while being chased by the police and smashed into a minivan carrying a family of four. All four members of the family were killed instantly. The driver of the car is brought by ambulance to the hospital. He has massive head injuries and requires quick and intensive treatment if he is going to live. The policeman who accompanies him explains to the emergency room staff that this man is wanted for murdering his own wife and child and led the police on a huge car chase through the city before crashing into the minivan. Maureen knows this man will surely die without her help. She thinks that she can save the man, but knows that nobody will know if she doesn't give her best effort and the man happens to die.

Discussion Questions:

1) What should Maureen do?

2) Is one human life ever less important than others?

3) Is not doing everything possible to save a human life the same thing as ending one?

4) If this person lives and goes on to kill again, is Maureen partially responsible?

We have discussed this Tough Choice.

_____

Parent/Guardian Signature

_____

Student Signature

SCIENCE & MEDICINE DILEMMA #3

Mrs. Terry had reminded the students to keep their goggles on throughout the entire lab period. She said if they needed to wipe them off, they must go to the hall and do this because of the dangers of getting chemicals in their eyes. She said it was especially dangerous for people who wear contact lenses because the contact lens can trap the chemical in the eye, preventing it from being washed away by tears. This results in damage to the eye.

Tim and Danny are lab partners in Mrs. Terry's chemistry class. One afternoon the two were conducting an experiment dealing with acids and bases. Tim took off his lab goggles because they were getting foggy. While he was wiping them off, something splashed out of a beaker and got in Tim's eye. Tim was obviously uncomfortable, but said that he was alright. Danny could see that Tim's eye was very red. Tim wears contact lenses.

Both students know that Tim will lose all of his lab points for removing his goggles during the lab. Tim does not want to tell Mrs. Terry, and he asks his friend Danny not to say anything either.

Discussion Questions:

1) Should Danny alert Mrs. Terry to the chemistry accident?

2) Would you have a different answer if Tim did not wear contact lenses?

3) How could this have been prevented?

We have discussed this Tough Choice.

_____   _____

Parent/Guardian Signature   Student Signature

SCIENCE & MEDICINE DILEMMA #4

Stanley and Tronesia just got married. They had genetic testing done, and have been informed that they are both carriers of the gene that codes for Tay-Sachs Disease. This means that although neither of them have the disease, they do have the instructions for the disease in their genome. There is a chance that these instructions could get passed on to their children. If they decide to have children, there is a 25 percent chance that each of their children will be afflicted with this disease.

There is no cure for Tay-Sachs Disease, and those who have it normally die by the time they are five years old. The disease results in the destruction of the nerve cells in the central nervous system. This causes a gradual deterioration of mental and motor skills, until death occurs. The bottom line is this is a horrible disease and the individual with the disease will endure much suffering, as will the parents who watch their child gradually die.

Discussion Questions:

1) Should Stanley and Tronesia attempt to have children?

2) Should this decision be allowed to be made by anyone other than the parents? For instance, should the government be able to pass a law preventing people in this situation from having children?

We have discussed this Tough Choice.

_____   _____

Parent/Guardian Signature   Student Signature

SCHOOL VIOLENCE DILEMMA #1

Early in his freshman year, Johnny was turned around on his way to class and came upon a part of school he had never been to before. As he tried to make his way through the crowd of students hanging out there, a fight broke out. Johnny had nothing to do with the fight and quickly moved out of the way and on to class, but not before seeing one boy throw a metal trashcan at the head of another. Several students identified Johnny at the scene.

Discussion Questions:

1) What should Johnny do?

2) If Johnny is sure he was not seen, should he definitely report the incident?

3) What if he believed someone could be seriously injured?

4) Who could Johnny tell?

We have discussed this Tough Choice.

_____   _____

Parent/Guardian Signature   Student Signature

SCHOOL VIOLENCE DILEMMA #2

   Although serious violence has not yet affected Quentin's school, there have been many bomb threats and rumors of violence occurring at other nearby schools. Last week while Quentin was at lunch, he overheard a conversation between a group of friends who were scheming to perform an act of violence on his school. In the midst of the conversation, they noticed Quentin watching and decided to continue the conversation elsewhere. Quentin wants to report them to a school authority, but he is worried that they will know that Quentin was the source since they saw him listening. However, he also feels a moral responsibility to speak up if lives could be at stake.

Discussion Questions:

1) Should Quentin confront that group directly?

2) If so, what should Quentin say to the group?

3) If they hurt anyone or do damage to the school, and Quentin does not tell, is he partially responsible?

4) What is your responsibility to your school, its students, and faculty?

We have discussed this Tough Choice.

_____   _____

Parent/Guardian Signature   Student Signature

SCHOOL VIOLENCE DILEMMA #3

Robbie is usually upset about something or another. When he isn't complaining about grades, it's the administration, jocks, or other students who kiss up to teachers. Margaret does not know Robbie well, but they sit next to one another in their last period of the day. Usually, Margaret thinks Robbie's complaints are funny, but lately he seems a little angrier than usual. He's been talking about a lack of respect and how much he hates the school.

Today, their class got back a research project, and Robbie received a low grade again. As they were leaving class, Robbie said to Margaret, "You know, that's it. These people don't know who they're dealing with. But after tomorrow . . . they'll know."

Discussion Questions:

1) What should Margaret do?

2) Should all threats of this kind be taken seriously? Why or why not?

3) What can schools do to prevent violent actions?

We have discussed this Tough Choice.

_____

Parent/Guardian Signature

_____

Student Signature

SPORTS & SPORTSMANSHIP DILEMMA #1

John's friend Terrell is extremely into sports. He has a dream of playing football in college someday. John has watched him workout every day over the summer and noticed that he has put on a tremendous amount of muscle. As the season is about to start, college scouts begin to visit and it seems that Terrell's dream may come true.

One day John is at Terrell's house, and Terrell asks him to get something from his desk in his room. Apparently John opens the wrong drawer in the desk, because what he is looking at is a bottle of steroids. Terrell sees what happened and tries to play it off. "It's not what you think," he says. "Coach gave them to a couple of us. They are brand new, so they aren't illegal yet. They're really helping me put on muscle!"

John cannot believe what he is hearing. Terrell is an intelligent guy and knows that he could be harming his body. John knows that steroids *are* illegal. He is very worried about his friend and the danger he is in. On the other hand, he doesn't want to get his friend in trouble, nor the whole football team, because most of the school would be mad at him. Terrell would be crushed because this might ruin his chance at playing in college.

Discussion Questions:

1) What should John do?

2) What does "being a friend" mean in this situation?

3) What advice would you give Terrell?

4) Should John limit his concern to his friend, or should it extend to the entire football program?

We have discussed this Tough Choice.

_____   _____
Parent/Guardian Signature   Student Signature

SPORTS & SPORTSMANSHIP DILEMMA #2

Sydney has a daughter that swims on the summer country club swim team. Every Wednesday night during the summer her daughter competes in a swim meet. For the last eight years, Sydney has volunteered to be a judge for the swim meets. She watches the swimmers to make sure that they do their strokes legally during the races. During the swim meet, Sydney is in charge of judging the opposing team's swimmers while the opposing team's judge watches Sydney's daughter's team's swimmers. At the last meet, Sydney was judging a race and noticed that a swimmer from her daughter's team made an illegal turn at the wall. However, the stroke judge responsible for the lane was not paying attention. Sydney was not responsible for watching the swimmer; she just happened to glance over and see the illegal turn.

Discussion Questions:

1) What should Sydney do?

2) Does Sydney have a responsibility to disqualify the swimmer?

3) Should Sydney act like nothing happened because she was not supposed to be looking at that lane anyway?

4) Would her decision change if her daughter was involved in the race?

5) What if her child was the one who made the illegal turn?

We have discussed this Tough Choice.

_____

Parent/Guardian Signature

_____

Student Signature

SPORTS & SPORTSMANSHIP DILEMMA #3

Trent is a senior at Johnson High School. He has been a member of the tennis team for four years and as a senior, he is captain and the number one single's player. Trent's senior tennis season has been quite successful. He has a 9-2 record, and he has helped his team to the first undefeated regular season in the school's history.

Trent eases through the regional tournament and goes on to the state tournament. At the state tournament, Trent wins his first two matches and makes it into the semifinals for the first time in his tennis career. The semifinal match is an extremely important match not only for the team but also for Trent, who could receive a college scholarship if he makes a good showing.

Trent's semifinal match is against a sophomore he has never played before. Trent wins the first set of the semifinal match 6-4. However, he falters in the second set and loses 3-6. The third set goes into a tiebreaker and Trent is down by one point with the match on the line. If he loses the point he will lose the match. However, if he wins the point he will be tied with a chance to still win the match. According to high school rules, the players make their own line calls during the match. There are no line judges. On match point, Trent's opponent hits a shot that is very close to being out of bounds and Trent cannot get to it in time to hit the shot back. At first, Trent is almost certain the shot was in, but it is close. He could very easily call the shot long and tie the game.

Discussion Questions:

1) What should Trent do?

2) Does Trent deserve the benefit of the doubt with the call because this is his last chance to compete in the state finals and his opponent will have two more years to compete?

3) Does Trent's call make that much of a difference since it is not a call that would win the game for him, just bring the score even?

4) Is there such a thing as "winning at all costs"?

We have discussed this Tough Choice.

_____   _____

Parent/Guardian Signature   Student Signature

SPORTS & SPORTSMANSHIP DILEMMA #4

John is a member of the baseball team at his school. He is the star pitcher, whom everyone counts on and looks up to. His team is playing against their archrival. In the second inning, John's teammate hits a home run off the opposing pitcher. When the same teammate comes up again to bat in the fifth inning, the opposing team's pitcher hits him in the head with a pitch. John's team is furious and John is sure the other team's pitcher was trying to get revenge for the home run that was hit earlier. Even John's coach is violently angry. He approaches John and gives him an order. The other team's pitcher is the second batter up the next time their team hits. The coach tells John to throw the ball at his head as payback for hitting John's teammate.

Discussion Questions:

1) What should John do?

2) What if the coach had not said to aim at the head but another part of the body?

3) At what point do the unwritten rules of sports (like retaliation pitches) get overruled by morality?

We have discussed this Tough Choice.

_____   _____

Parent/Guardian Signature   Student Signature

STUDENT LIFE DILEMMA #1

Bretia has been friends with Tomeka since fifth grade and they have always planned on double dating for their senior prom. Bretia has befriended Fred, basically a good kid but also thought of by people as "annoying". It is a week before prom and there are several couples planning on going to dinner and a boat ride before prom. Fred asks Bretia if he can come along and bring his date. Bretia knows that Tomeka really doesn't like Fred and the other couples aren't that close with him but she also knows that Fred is a sweet kid who has a nice date. Tomeka has allowed some of the other couples to come along without consulting Bretia.

Discussion Questions:

1) What should Bretia do?

2) Suppose everyone decides that they would rather not have Fred along?

3) What if Tomeka suggests that, if Fred comes with them, then Bretia wouldn't be welcome at her house-party afterwards?

4) What if everyone says "no" to Fred but Fred says that he can get free limousines through his uncle for everyone that goes together?

We have discussed this Tough Choice.

_____   _____

Parent/Guardian Signature   Student Signature

STUDENT LIFE DILEMMA #2

Jason is a junior in high school with some special academic needs. It is understood and accepted by all that Jason takes longer on tests and gets extra help after school from his teachers. Jason is very friendly to everyone but some students like to pick on him because of his learning challenges. Lauren is a classmate of Jason's and frequently hangs out with a large group of friends. She is not particularly close to Jason, nor does she know him that well. One day after school, Lauren sees a group of her friends pushing Jason in the hall calling him "retard" and "freak".

Discussion Questions:

1) What should Lauren do?

2) Does she have a Christian duty to help Jason?

3) What does Lauren risk if she stands up to her friends?

4) What could Lauren say to her friends?

We have discussed this Tough Choice.

_____   _____

Parent/Guardian Signature   Student Signature

STUDENT LIFE DILEMMA #3

Kevin is a freshman at a state college. He is very knowledgeable about computers. For his graduation from high school his parents gave him a very sophisticated computer, which includes a scanner and photo-editing capabilities. During his first weeks of college, Kevin figures out that his computer coupled with his knowledge can make him some extra spending money if he makes fake identification cards for his dorm mates. He is aware that making fake ID's is a crime, but he doesn't think there is any way he can be caught.

Discussion Questions:

1) What should Kevin do?

2) Should Kevin's decision be based on whether or not he thinks he will be caught?

3) Would this action be correct if Kevin planned to donate all of his money to charity?

We have discussed this Tough Choice.

_____

Parent/Guardian Signature

_____

Student Signature

STUDENT LIFE DILEMMA #4

Katie and Betsy are at the movies, early on a Saturday afternoon. As the movie ends, they notice that a few other classmates had been watching the same movie in the theater. They begin talking and Katie mentions that the two of them have no plans for the rest of the day. She inquires about what the other classmates are doing after the movie. The others say that they are going to stay in the theater complex all day, hopping in and out of different theaters, and seeing other movies for free. They invite Katie and Betsy to join them, since the girls said that they had no prior plans.

Discussion Questions:

1) What should the girls do?

2) What would you say to someone who said, "The movie theater isn't going to miss a few dollars. Besides, nobody was going to sit in that seat anyway."?

3) Would this action be considered stealing?

We have discussed this Tough Choice.

_____

Parent/Guardian Signature

_____

Student Signature

STUDENT LIFE DILEMMA #5

Matt, Brian, Jason, and Chris all grew up on the same street. They are juniors in high school. Together the boys have formed a close-knit group. On the corner of their street lives a crotchety, elderly gentleman, Mr. Ebert. He is notorious for yelling at the children whenever they play ball in the street because he thinks they block the road. Whenever the boys would hit a ball into his yard, he would keep it. Recently, Brian lost a soccer ball to Mr. Ebert and Chris a new football. Both boys are very upset and decide that on Halloween they are going to give Mr. Ebert something else to keep. They plan on throwing some eggs on his property. Brian and Chris go to the grocery store and buy two dozen eggs.

On Halloween night, when the four boys come to the end of the street, near Mr. Ebert's house, Brian and Chris inform the other two of their plan to egg the house. Matt, who once lost a basketball to Mr. Ebert, thinks this is a good idea. Jason is not so sure. Because of his uncertainty, the others tease him for awhile. Chris finally suggests that if Jason does not want to throw any eggs, then at least he can serve as a "lookout" to make sure nobody sees the boys vandalizing the house.

Discussion Questions:

1) What should Jason do?

2) Should Jason continue walking with the boys and act as a lookout?

3) If Jason just stands as "look out" is he as guilty as the rest?

4) Is there another way to solve the problem with Mr. Ebert?

We have discussed this Tough Choice.

_____   _____

Parent/Guardian Signature   Student Signature

STUDENT LIFE DILEMMA #6

At 11 p.m., Mary is driving home in her neighborhood from a friend's house. In a split second, a dog runs out in front of her car and she hits the dog. Mary gets out and sees that the dog is dead. She looks at the dog's collar and sees the owner of the dog lives a few houses down. No one is around and no one saw the accident.

Discussion Questions:

1) What should she do?

2) What if Mary hit a person?

3) What if the dog didn't have a collar?

4) What if Mary had been drinking?

We have discussed this Tough Choice.

_____   _____

Parent/Guardian Signature   Student Signature

ACKNOWLEDGMENTS

We would like to thank the following people for all of their help, support, and encouragement:

Our families, for our upbringing, ideas for this book, and suggestions on revisions.

Our colleagues for their ideas, submission of dilemma entries, and/or editorial skills, namely: Dan McCue, Scott Bishop, Scott Reis, Max Engel, Mike Faggella, Julie Tilghman, Mark Low, Danny Easley, Patricia Sevilla, Gina Navoa, Andrea Ray-Alessio, Mary Kate Pilcher, and Sean Macmanus.

Fr. Timothy R. Scully, C.S.C., Dr. John Staud, Dr. Joyce V. Johnstone, Dr. Thomas Doyle, Dr. G. Michael Pressley, Dr. F. Clark Power, and the members, faculty, and staff of the Alliance for Catholic Education Program.

Mr. Steve Ritterbush, for his continuous dedication and philanthropy in support of new ideas in Catholic education.

Dr. Thomas Lickona, whose guest lecture in a summer class planted the seed for this endeavor and whose support and suggestions have been instrumental along the way.

The administration, faculty, staff, parents, and students of both Bishop Sullivan High School in Baton Rouge, LA and Bishop Kelley High School in Tulsa, OK, who allowed this idea to be tried in the classrooms and who supported its development.

Mr. Bob Hamma and Mr. Mike Amodei at Ave Maria Press for their interest, suggestions, and assistance in the development of this book.

Sean Lynch coordinates the Alliance for Catholic Education educational outreach program at the University of Notre Dame. A former high school teacher at Bishop Sullivan High School in Baton Rouge, Louisiana, Lynch is a 1998 graduate of the University of Notre Dame. He received his Masters of Education from Notre Dame in 2000.

Brian O'Brien is currently studying for the priesthood for the diocese of Tulsa, Oklahoma at St. Meinrad's School of Theology. O'Brien previously taught theology at Bishop Kelley High School in Tulsa. He has a Bachelor of Arts degree in theology and political science from Boston College and a Masters of Education from Notre Dame.